BRICK
ROBOTS

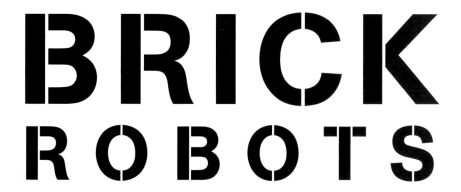

BRICK
ROBOTS

AN UNOFFICIAL GUIDE TO MAKING 30 AWESOME ROBOTS
FROM CLASSIC LEGO®

KEVIN HALL

BARRON'S

First edition for the United States and Canada
published in 2018 by Barron's Educational Series, Inc.

All inquiries should be addressed to:
Barron's Educational Series, Inc.
250 Wireless Boulevard
Hauppauge, NY 11788
www.barronseduc.com

Library of Congress Control Number: 2018936895
ISBN 978-1-4380-1197-4

This book was conceived, designed, and produced by
The Bright Press, an imprint of the Quarto Group
The Old Brewery, 6 Blundell Street,
London N7 9BH, United Kingdom

Publisher: Mark Searle
Associate Publisher: Emma Bastow
Creative Director: James Evans
Commissioning Editor: Sorrel Wood
Managing Editor: Isheeta Mustafi
Designer: Tony Seddon
Editors: Rica Dearman, Abbie Sharman

9 8 7 6 5 4 3 2 1

Printed in Malaysia

About the authors

Kevin Hall is a cofounder of Brick Galleria—a LEGO® brick
model building design and events company—and a professional
LEGO brick artist. He designs, develops, and creates LEGO brick
models for companies, events, promotions, and collectors. He
has been part of the international LEGO community since 2000,
creating models and sculptures and designing custom collector
figurines, bespoke sets, graphics, and promotional material for
events around the world. His models have been featured in
television advertising campaigns, toy fairs, exhibitions, print
media, and theme parks, and have been used by government
organizations. He recently turned his hand to writing and his
work was featured in the official LEGO book, *365 Things to Do
with LEGO Bricks*, which won the "Best Book" category in the
Creative Play Awards 2016 in the United Kingdom. He also
organizes and runs LEGO workshops for children and corporate
groups. Before becoming a professional LEGO brick artist,
Kevin spent three decades in the advertising industry in various
creative incarnations.

Brenda Tsang is a cofounder of Brick Galleria. This followed
15 years of creating and managing products for global
entertainment brands. Brenda is passionate about creating
products that have cutting-edge functionality, are aesthetically
pleasing, and stand out from the crowd. She also specializes in
scenery art and spatial design, which enables her to create the
enhanced experience of Brick Galleria events. Brenda helped
on the research and design for models in this book and with
selecting LEGO parts for some of the finer details.

William Wong assists with Brick Galleria, helping to set up
exhibitions as well as create models, as he has done for this
book. He has been an active member of the international LEGO
community for the past decade and displays his models all
around the world. William is also a marketing consultant and
uses his knowledge to help with organizing events. His attention
to detail means his models are very intricate and imaginative,
as you can see in this book.

contents

A word from the author

A lot of the time when I am at an event displaying my LEGO® brick models, I am asked if my models and sculptures are created using special parts, or if I get unique parts made especially for a particular model. The answer is that the parts I use are the exact same parts that you get in the LEGO sets you purchase in stores. This book aims to show precisely that.

All the models in this book have been created using the basic parts that you will find in the CLASSIC boxes, which of course aren't just classic 2 × 4 bricks, but include slopes, plates, and tiles.

When I am building my models, I always love the challenge of creating a model using the parts I have at hand. So, don't worry if you haven't got the exact pieces I list. Just like any LEGO builder, you can be creative and recreate the models in this book to suit the parts you have in your own collection. Remember, there is no right or wrong way of building with LEGO, as long as you have fun creating the models. That is the most important thing.

—Kevin Hall, Brick Galleria Ltd

The robot characters that appear in this book are purely fictional and have been invented specifically for this book. Any resemblance to other robot characters is purely coincidental.

How to use this book

Brick Robots contains 30 different models that you can build out of LEGO® pieces. They are easy to build—and lots of fun!

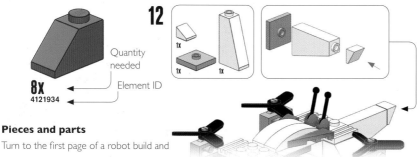

Quantity needed

Element ID

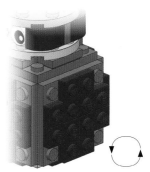

Pieces and parts

Turn to the first page of a robot build and you'll see a picture of the model you're going to build, plus a short introduction. Below this, you'll see a pictorial list of all the LEGO pieces required to build this robot. The quantity needed sits below the piece, and below this is the element ID.

Following the instructions

Once you have gathered all of the pieces required for a build, start to create your robot following the step-by-step instructions on the pages that follow. Each step contains a materials box that shows the pieces needed for that step.

For complex builds, you will also find an additional instruction box showing how the pieces are to be put together—some have red arrows to show you exactly how to connect the pieces to each other, while others will also have black arrows to show you where to place them on the build. (See above.)

Work your way through all of the steps. You'll then have your completed robot and should have used up all the pieces that appeared in the initial list.

Note

Look out for the round symbol with arrows (see above) on some of the builds—it means that you need to rotate the robot as you make it.

It couldn't be simpler than that!

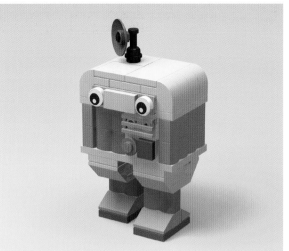

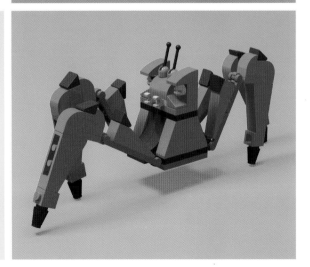

Brains

This intelligent robot is a multitasking professional. Its large hands mean it can juggle several tasks simultaneously. While most creatures' brains are located in their heads, this robot's genius lies within the magnetic coils in the front of its chest. Create the coils by mixing three red- and three green-colored transparent round plates. Use 2 × 2 round bricks with flutes to give Brains' legs and arms a retro look.

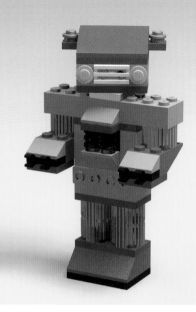

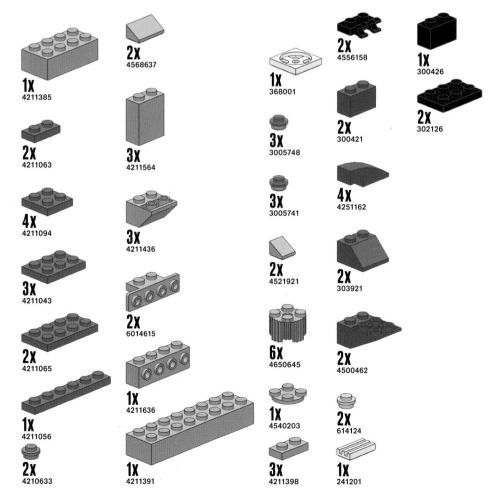

1x
4211385

2x
4568637

2x
4211063

3x
4211564

4x
4211094

3x
4211436

3x
4211043

2x
6014615

2x
4211065

1x
4211636

1x
4211056

2x
4210633

1x
4211391

1x
368001

3x
3005748

3x
3005741

2x
4521921

6x
4650645

1x
4540203

3x
4211398

2x
4556158

2x
300421

4x
4251162

2x
303921

2x
4500462

2x
614124

1x
241201

1x
300426

2x
302126

BRAINS

1

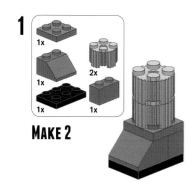

1x
1x
1x
2x
1x

MAKE 2

2

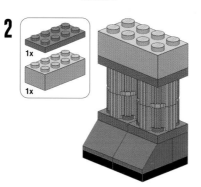

1x
1x

3

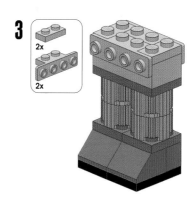

2x
2x

4

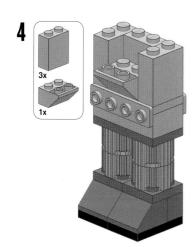

3x
1x

5

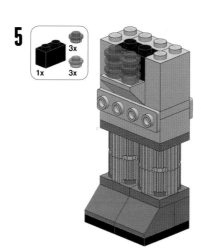

3x
1x
3x

6

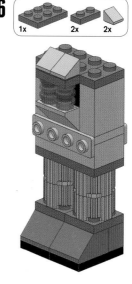

1x
2x
2x

7

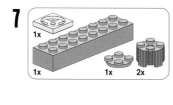

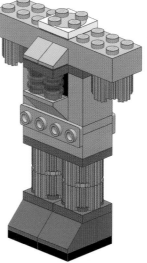

1x
1x
1x
2x

8

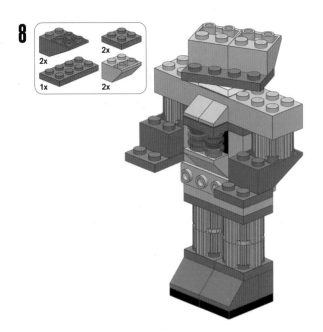

9

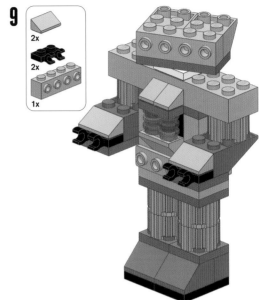

10

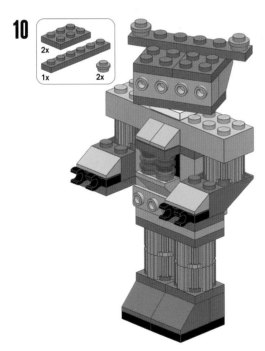

11

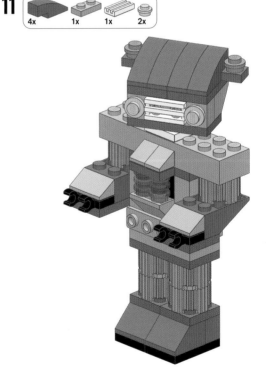

SparkZ

SparkZ is designed to be the best robotic server, and you can build it with just a small collection of bricks. Use 1 x 2 plates with a handle on the side to hold the serving trays, and use any kind of brick you like for the drinks it is holding. Connect the legs to a 2 x 2 octagonal plate with bar frame, which makes up the midsection of the body. Attach the two arms to this central piece.

1x
4211183

3x
4515364

7x
4540040

2x
306223

3x
4273590

1x
4221775

1x
6009016

1x
403224

4x
4583862

1x
4653822

1x
4210633

1x
3006343

3x
4535740

1x
4649773

2x
4515350

1x
6023173

1x
3006844

2x
6099548

2x
4226876

2x
6136419

1x
618847

2x
403201

3x
4619599

SPARKZ

1 1x 1x 1x

2 3x 3x 3x 3x 1 2 3x

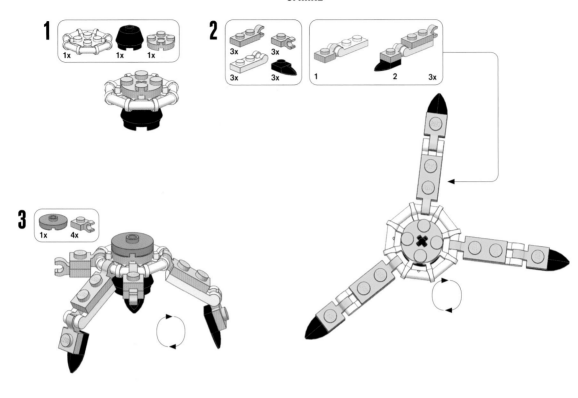

3 1x 4x

4 2x 2x

5 1x 1x 2x

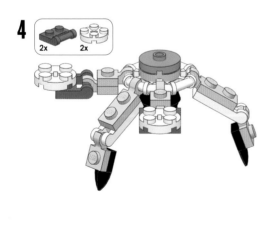

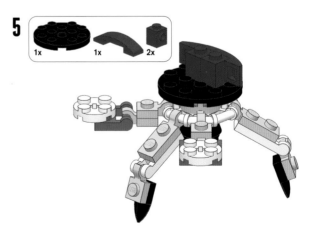

6 2x

7 2x 2x

8 1x 1x

9 1x 1x

10 1x 1x 3x 1x 1x 1x

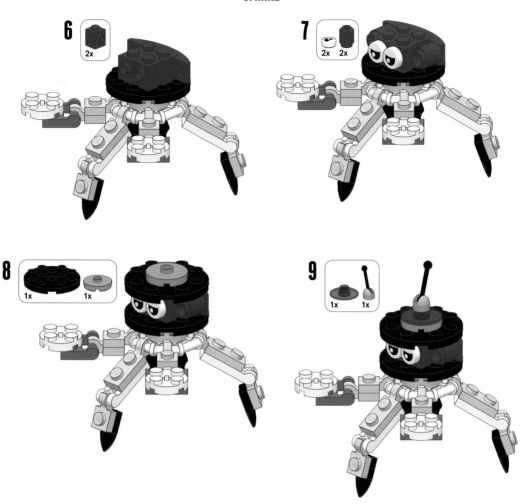

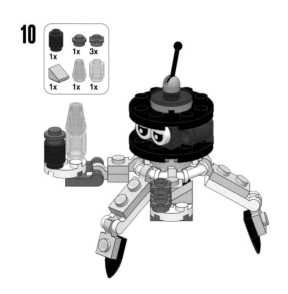

BuzzER

Resembling a small flying insect, BuzzER is a cute little critter with big buglike eyes. Use 2 × 2 red-colored transparent radar dishes with 1 × 1 round plates set inside them for its large eyes. Small levers are perfect for the antennae, and an inverted slope gives the impression it has a tummy. Connect 1 × 1 plates with a clip to 1 × 2 plates with a handle on the end for its wings. You can build the BuzzER robot in the following 10 simple steps.

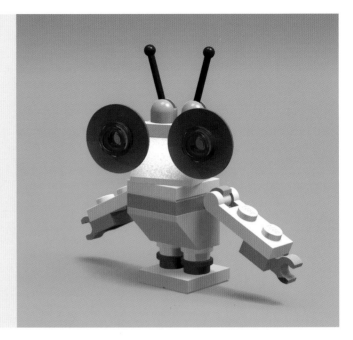

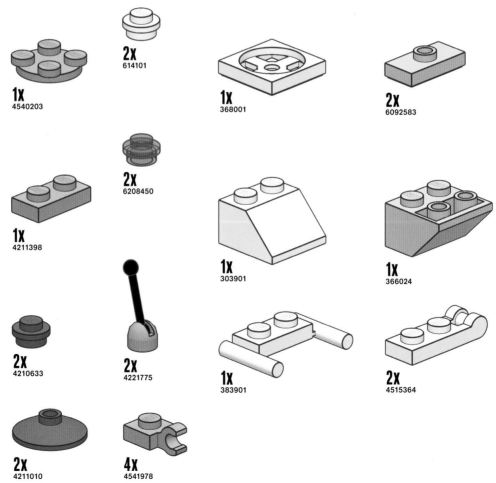

1x
4540203

2x
614101

1x
368001

2x
6092583

1x
4211398

2x
6208450

1x
303901

1x
366024

2x
4210633

2x
4221775

1x
383901

2x
4515364

2x
4211010

4x
4541978

BUZZER

1

2

3

4

5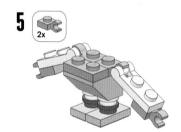

6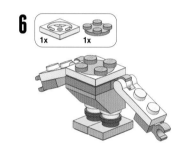

7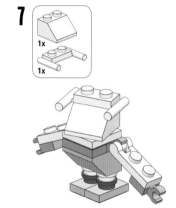

8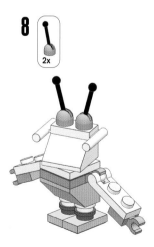

9

10

15

Gearbox

Gearbox is your friendly neighborhood fix-it bot. You can build it in any color combination, but we've chosen different hues of blue. This robot is made up mostly of square bricks, but rounded elements and movable parts soften its appearance. For the base of the body, use a 1 × 2 brick with a handle, which allows for 1 × 1 plates with horizontal clips to be attached to create the feet. Attach the eyes to 1 × 1 bricks with a stud on the side.

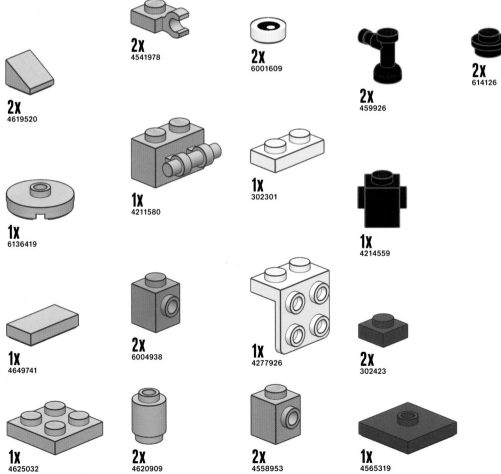

2x 4619520

2x 4541978

2x 6001609

2x 459926

2x 614126

1x 6136419

1x 4211580

1x 302301

1x 4214559

1x 4649741

2x 6004938

1x 4277926

2x 302423

1x 4625032

2x 4620909

2x 4558953

1x 4565319

GEARBOX

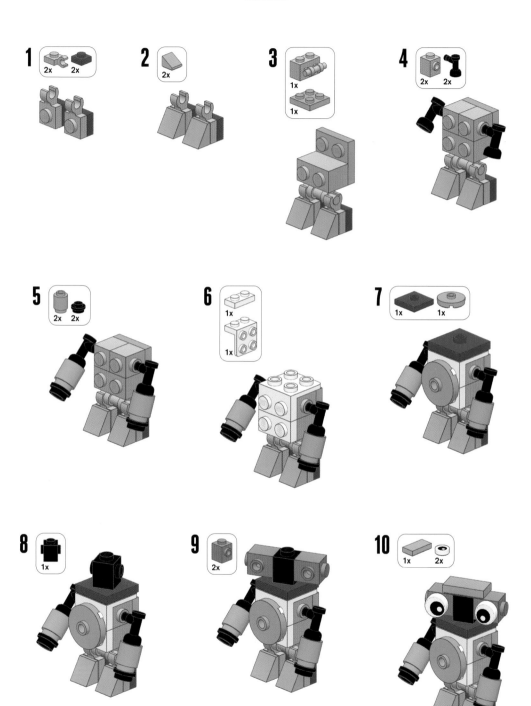

Auto 4

Auto 4 is a compact, traditional robot created to assist humans—its role could be to help with household chores, which is why it resembles a timeless sci-fi character from an old movie. Use different-sized radar dishes to make a great base, and then connect a plate with a clip to a plate with a handle so that the body can lean forward or backward. Tooth plates give Auto 4 its ears, and 1 × 1 plates with clip pieces make ideal hands.

1x
6023173

1x
4222017

1x
4180087

2x
4224792

1x
6073042

2x
6240214

2x
302424

1x
614126

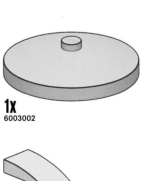
1x
6003002

1x
4211010

4x
4540040

1x
4598528

1x
6147726

3x
4521187

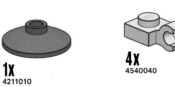
1x
4547489

1x
4535739

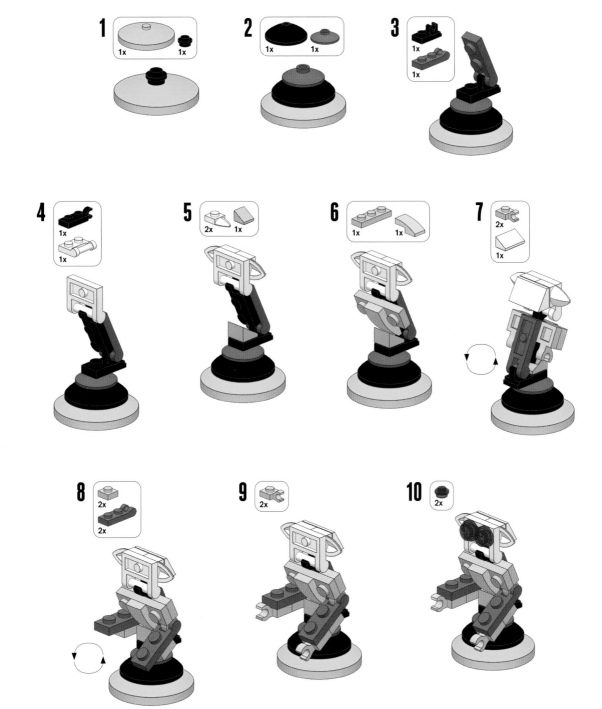

Microcontroller

Microcontroller has four legs, which help it to multitask. Build this spiderlike robot out of some of the more unusual LEGO® bricks. Start with its center, then add on the legs and finally its head. Create each leg using 1 × 2 plates with a horizontal clip on the end and 1 × 2 plates with a handle on the end to allow the legs to bend. Place 1 × 1 round plates between other bricks to create this creature's "evil" stare.

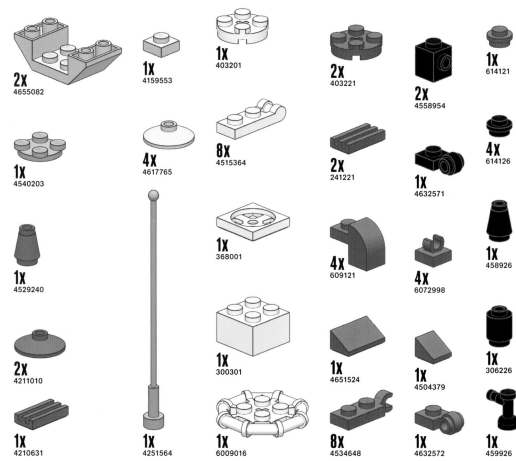

2x 4655082

1x 4159553

1x 403201

2x 403221

2x 4558954

1x 614121

1x 4540203

4x 4617765

8x 4515364

2x 241221

1x 4632571

4x 614126

1x 4529240

1x 368001

4x 609121

4x 6072998

1x 458926

2x 4211010

1x 300301

1x 4651524

1x 4504379

1x 306226

1x 4210631

1x 4251564

1x 6009016

8x 4534648

1x 4632572

1x 459926

MICROCONTROLLER

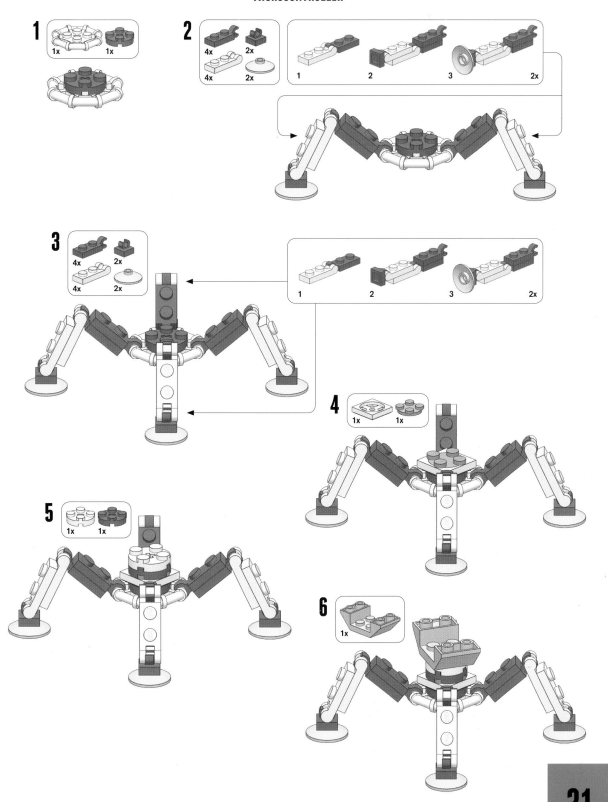

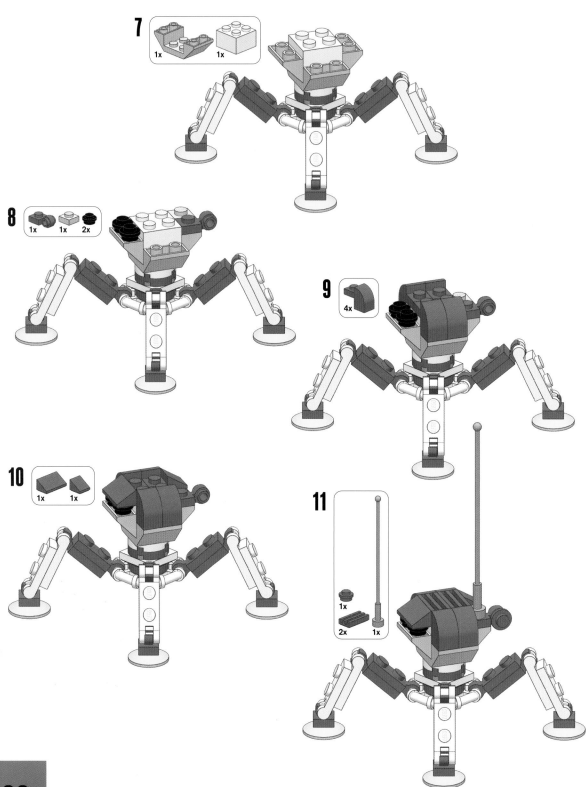

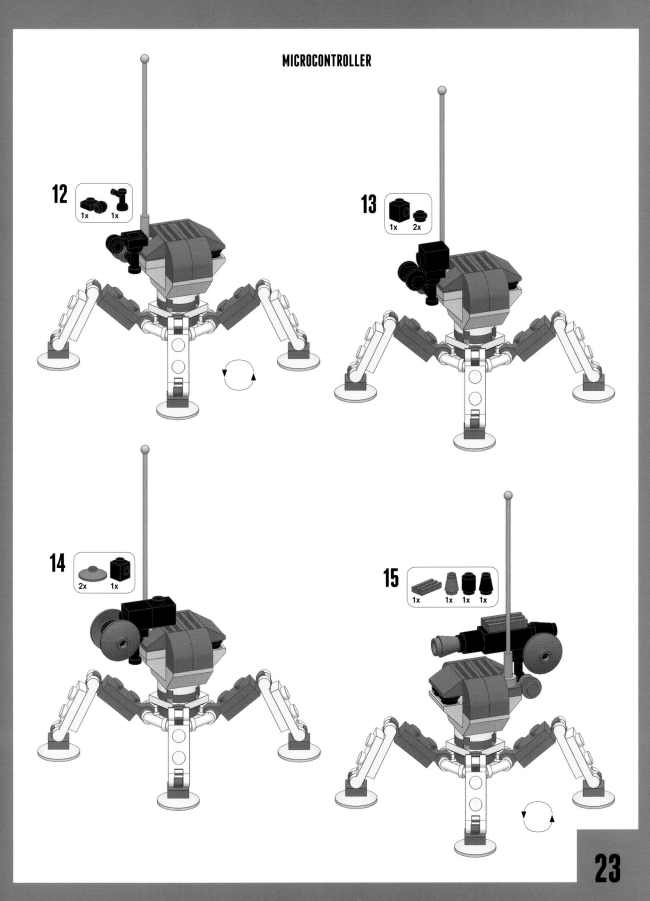

RADstinger

This little critter resembles a scorpion—when its long tail is positioned upward, as in this picture, the sting on its end is visible. Both the tail and legs use plates with clips and bars, which allow them to hinge and move. Use a ball and socket joint to allow the head to be angled in all directions. You can experiment with different-colored bricks to create a different-looking RADstinger.

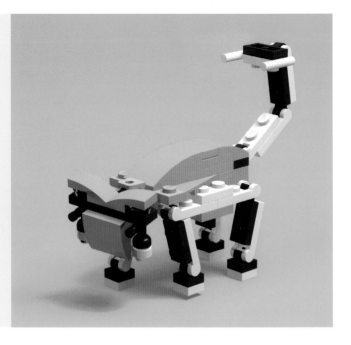

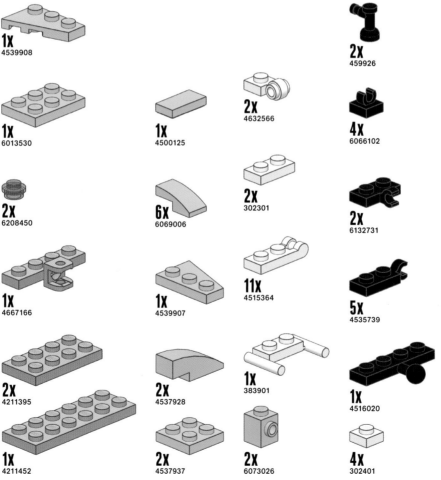

1x 4539908

2x 459926

1x 6013530

1x 4500125

2x 4632566

4x 6066102

2x 6208450

6x 6069006

2x 302301

2x 6132731

1x 4667166

1x 4539907

11x 4515364

5x 4535739

2x 4211395

2x 4537928

1x 383901

1x 4516020

1x 4211452

2x 4537937

2x 6073026

4x 302401

RADSTINGER

1
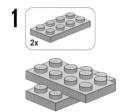

2
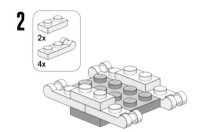

3
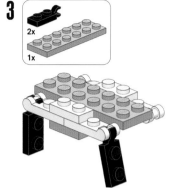

4
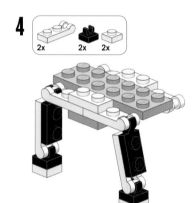

5

6
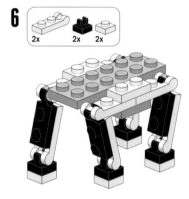

7
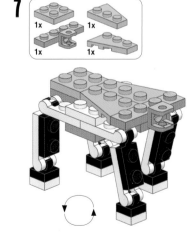

8
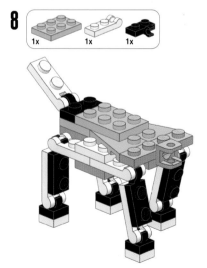

9

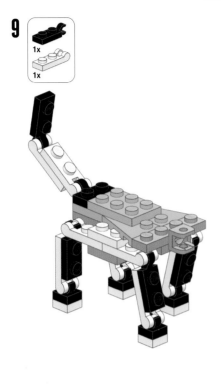

10

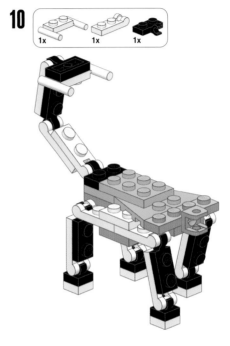

11

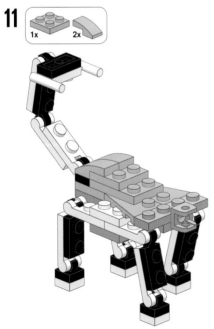

12

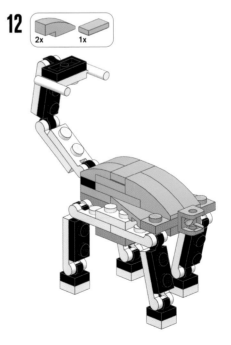

13

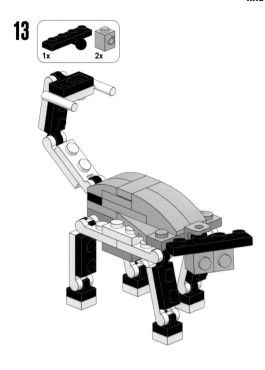

14

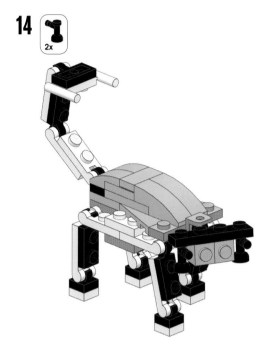

15

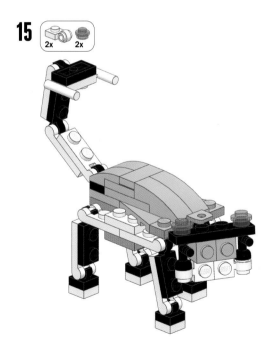

16

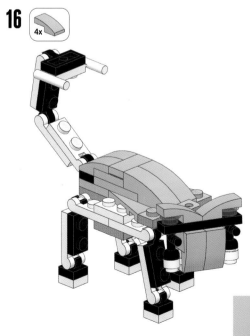

Drillbit

This handy robot is a busy little worker on wheels. It likes to help out wherever it can—it uses its hook to tow broken-down vehicles to a garage, or transport building supplies around construction sites. Build your version of Drillbit by attaching the hook to the arm using a hinge and towball socket piece. Use a 2 × 2 turntable on the rear set of wheels to allow the robot to steer. Click hinges mean the head can move up and down as needed.

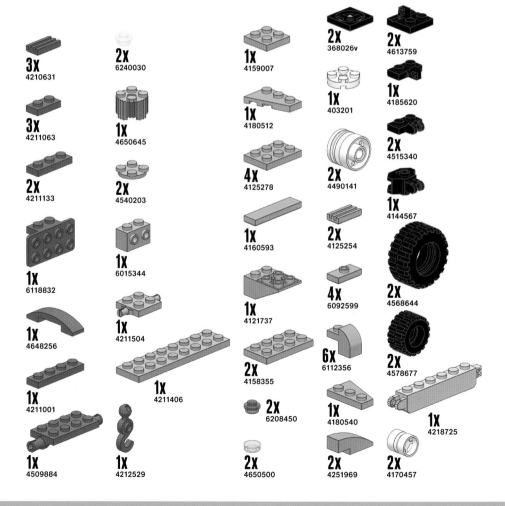

3X
4210631

2X
6240030

1X
4159007

2X
368026v

2X
4613759

3X
4211063

1X
4650645

1X
4180512

1X
403201

1X
4185620

2X
4211133

2X
4540203

4X
4125278

2X
4490141

2X
4515340

1X
6118832

1X
6015344

1X
4160593

2X
4125254

1X
4144567

1X
4648256

1X
4211504

1X
4121737

4X
6092599

2X
4568644

1X
4211001

1X
4211406

2X
4158355

6X
6112356

2X
4578677

2X
6208450

1X
4180540

1X
4218725

1X
4509884

1X
4212529

2X
4650500

2X
4251969

2X
4170457

DRILLBIT

1
1x
1x
1x
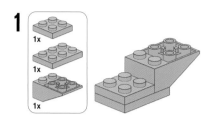

2
1x
1x
1x
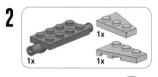
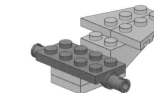

3
2x
1x
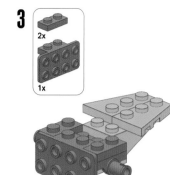

4
2x
1x
1x
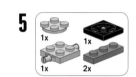
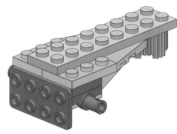

5
1x
1x
1x
2x
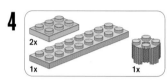
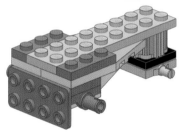

6
1x
2x
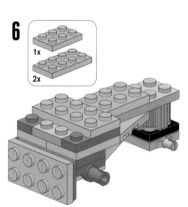

7
4x
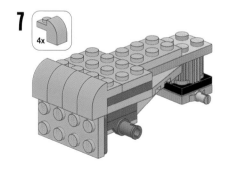

8
4x
1x
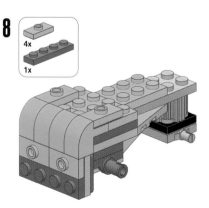

DRILLBIT

9

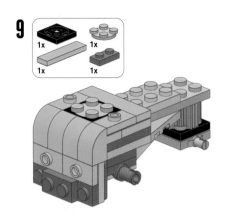

10

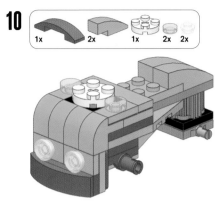

11

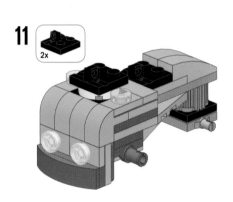

12

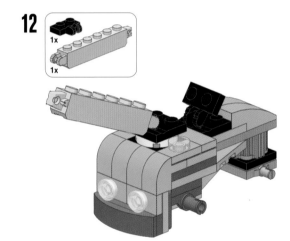

13

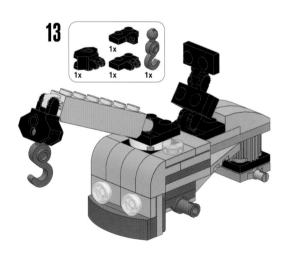

14

2x

1x

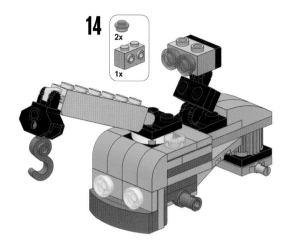

15

2x

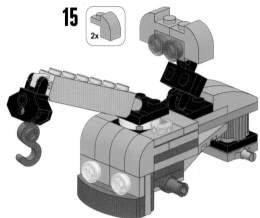

16

3x

2x

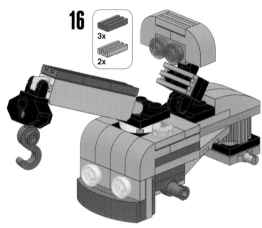

17

2x

2x

2x

2x

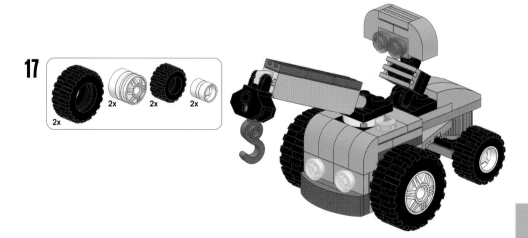

Dataroid

Dataroid is an alien robot, far away from its home planet. Build your own brick version with movable parts. Create its space helmet head using two 4 x 4 radar dishes with the bottom one upside down. Connect the legs and arms to the body using 1 x 1 tap pieces—these allow the limbs to be rotated up and down as well as side to side. Use levers for its antennae so that Dataroid can pick up signals from passing spaceships and find its way back home.

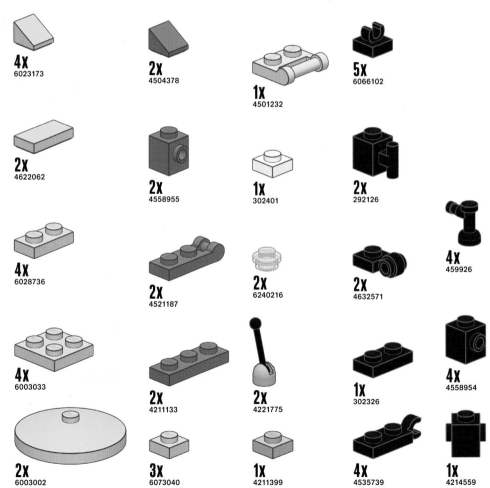

4x 6023173

2x 4504378

1x 4501232

5x 6066102

2x 4622062

2x 4558955

1x 302401

2x 292126

4x 6028736

2x 4521187

2x 6240216

2x 4632571

4x 459926

4x 6003033

2x 4211133

2x 4221775

1x 302326

4x 4558954

2x 6003002

3x 6073040

1x 4211399

4x 4535739

1x 4214559

DATAROID

1 2x 4x

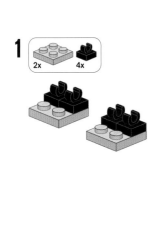

2 2x 4x

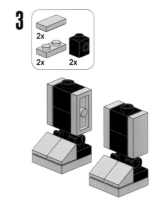

3 2x 2x 2x

4 1x 2x 2x

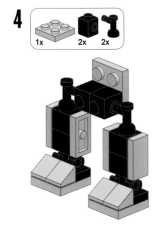

5 2x 2x

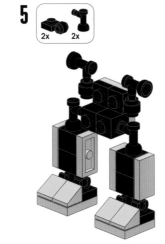

6 1x 1x

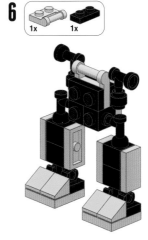

7 2x 2x 1x 2x

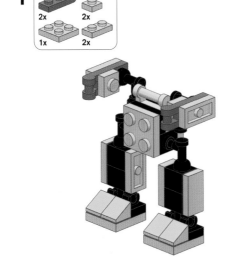

8 4x

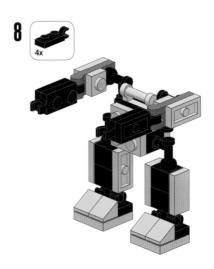

DATAROID

9

1x

10
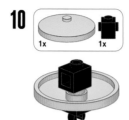
1x   1x

11
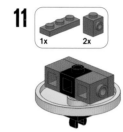
1x   2x

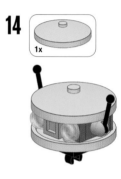

12
2x   1x
1x   1x

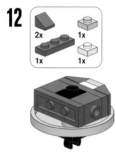

13
2x   1x
1x   2x

14
1x

15

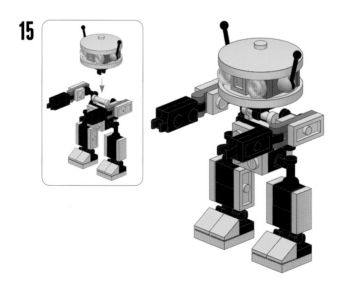

Wires

Wires is probably the best-dressed robot you'll ever come across, with a new outfit for every occasion. Aside from the sharp suit, its hat matches the shoes worn on its incredibly large feet. Build the base of this robot's torso using 1 x 1 bricks with a stud on the side so the legs can be attached using 1 x 1 clips. Use grille tiles for the ruffle feature of its shirt, and connect these to the torso using a bracket piece.

1x
6174640

2x
6063897

4x
4515364

2x
241201

2x
302326

1x
614126

3x
4622062

2x
6092604

1x
302201

2x
302301

2x
4535739

4x
6066102

2x
6122504

2x
4566607

2x
366001

2x
366501

2x
302401

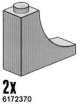
2x
6172370

1x
4659770

1x
371001

2x
300401

2x
4504369

1x
6003033

6x
6035470

2x
6208450

3x
4277926

3x
4558952

35

WIRES

1
2x 2x 2x
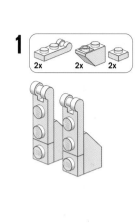

2
2x 2x 2x

3
2x

4
1x 1x 2x
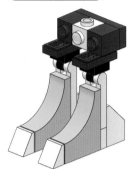

5
3x
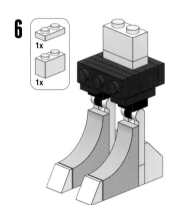

6
1x 1x

7
2x 1x
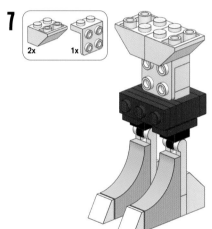

8
2x 1x 1x
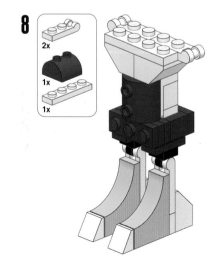

9
2x 2x
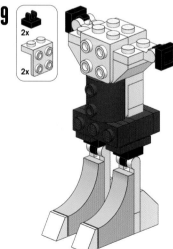

10
2x 2x
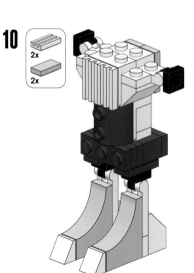

WIRES

11

2x
2x

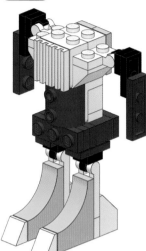

12

2x
2x

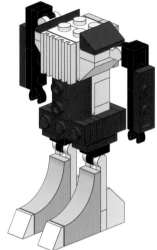

13

1x 1x

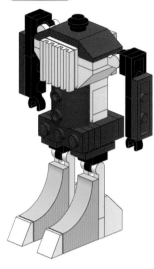

14
1x 1x 1x

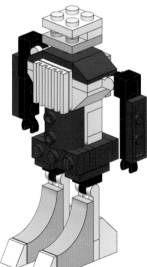

15
1x 2x

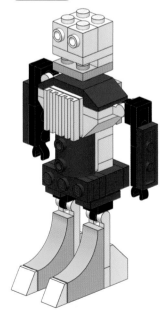

16
2x 1x 2x

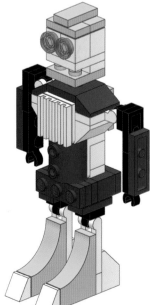

Tronical

This robot is a friendly flying machine. Its mission is search and rescue—it has a giant torch attached to the underside of its body to help it locate missing robots, and always has one eye wide open on the lookout. Build your own Tronical using a turntable for the torch so that it can swivel from side to side. Attach the rotor blade assemblies using 2 × 2 × 2/3 plates with studs on the side, and 2 × 2 plates with a wheel holder.

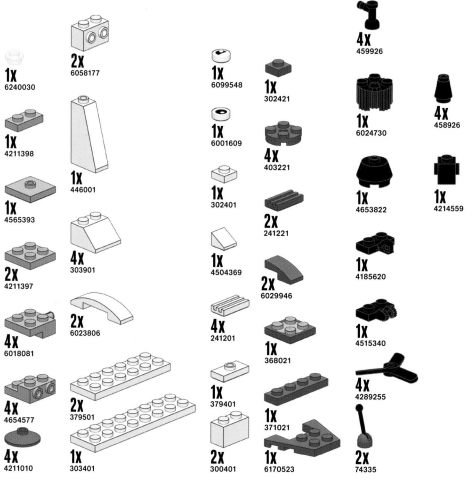

1x 6240030

2x 6058177

1x 4211398

1x 446001

1x 4565393

2x 4211397

4x 303901

4x 6018081

2x 6023806

4x 4654577

2x 379501

4x 4211010

1x 303401

1x 6099548

1x 302421

1x 6001609

4x 403221

1x 302401

2x 241221

1x 4504369

2x 6029946

4x 241201

1x 368021

1x 379401

1x 371021

2x 300401

1x 6170523

4x 459926

1x 6024730

4x 458926

1x 4653822

1x 4214559

1x 4185620

1x 4515340

4x 4289255

2x 74335

TRONICAL

1
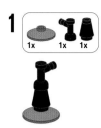
1x 1x 1x

2

1x

3

1x

4

1x
1x
MAKE 4

5
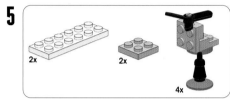
2x 2x 4x

6

1x
1x

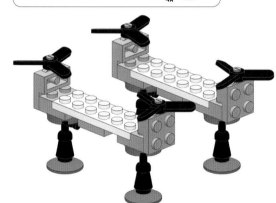

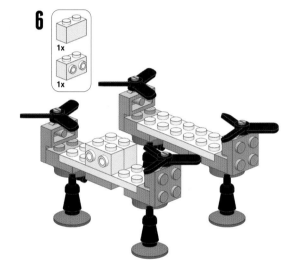

7
1x
1x

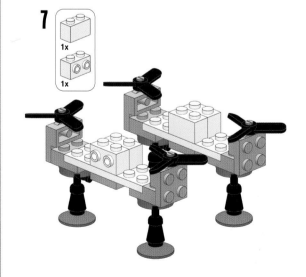

8
4x

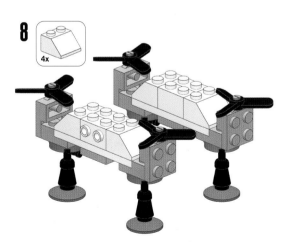

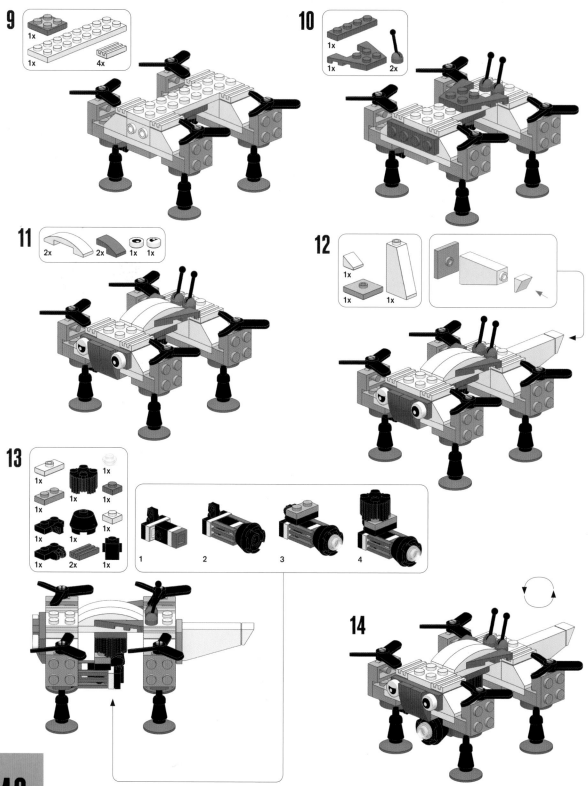

9
1x
1x
4x

10
1x
1x
2x

11
2x
2x
1x
1x

12
1x
1x
1x

13
1x
1x
1x
1x
1x
1x
1x
2x
1x

1
2
3
4

14

Blue

This blue beast is an eco-warrior that likes to consume plastic trash. It has big wheels just like a dune buggy, and the beach is its favorite place to find plastic litter. It rolls over the sand and uses its big hands to pick up the plastic, which it then places inside a compartment in its head. Build your brick Blue robot using a turntable—this will allow the body to swivel around. Create movable arms by connecting click hinges and plates with clips and handles.

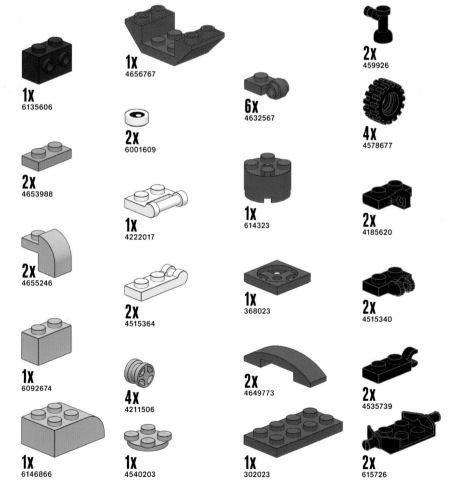

1x 6135606

1x 4656767

2x 459926

2x 4653988

2x 6001609

6x 4632567

4x 4578677

2x 4655246

1x 4222017

1x 614323

2x 4185620

2x 4515364

1x 368023

2x 4515340

1x 6092674

4x 4211506

2x 4649773

2x 4535739

1x 6146866

1x 4540203

1x 302023

2x 615726

BLUE

1
2x
1x

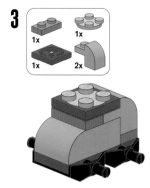

2
1x 1x

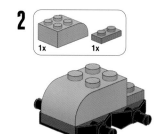

3
1x 1x
1x 2x

4
1x 1x

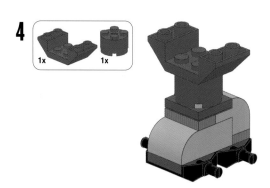

5
1x
1x

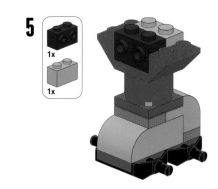

6
2x 2x 2x

7
2x
2x

8

2x
1x
2x

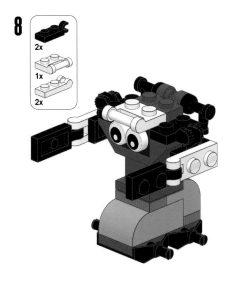

9

2x

10

4x

11

4x 4x

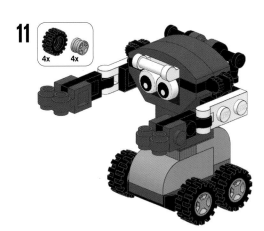

Time-O

The groovy-looking Time-O is visiting us from the future—and boy does it like to party! It's got lime-green dancing shoes on and its mouth is open, ready to sing. Create your LEGO® Time-O using clip pieces for hands that are clicking along in time to the music. Use a transparent 2 × 2 round brick with a 2 × 2 dome brick on top for the robot's head, and attach the antennae to 1 × 1 clip plates for its skinny legs.

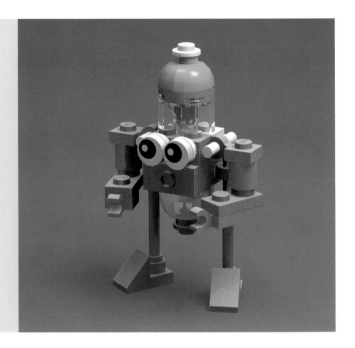

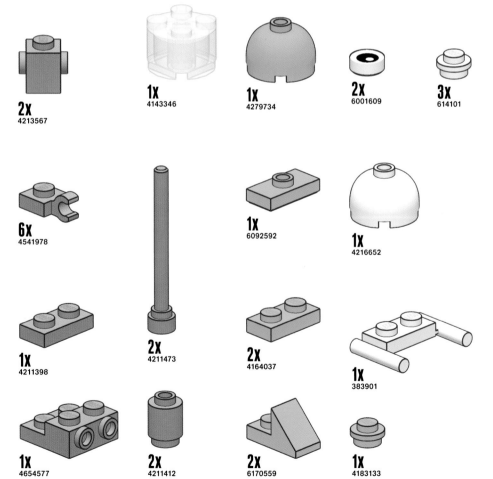

2x 4213567

1x 4143346

1x 4279734

2x 6001609

3x 614101

6x 4541978

1x 6092592

1x 4216652

1x 4211398

2x 4211473

2x 4164037

1x 383901

1x 4654577

2x 4211412

2x 6170559

1x 4183133

TIME-O

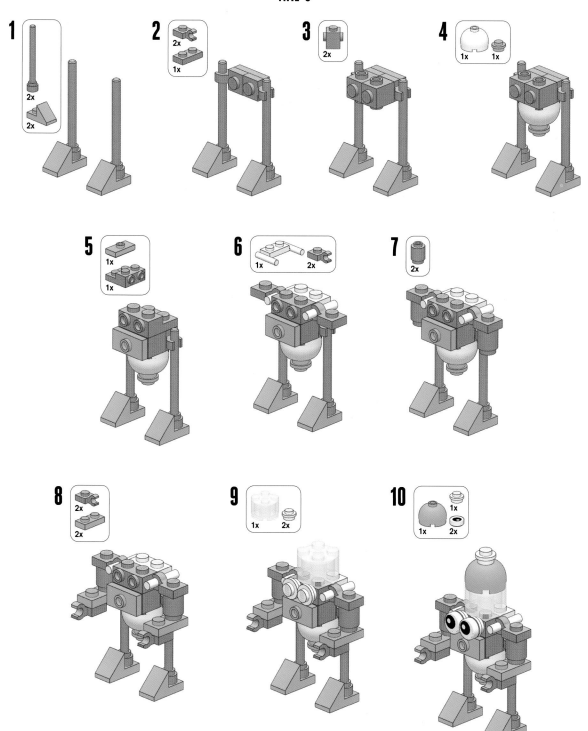

Sprite

Sprite likes to play tricks on everyone—and usually gets away with them due to its innocent appearance. It wears a bow in its long hair, but it's the winking eye that gives the game away. Build the main body of this robot with a 1 × 1 brick with studs on each side, and attach the arms. Connect tooth plates to a corner plate to make the feet point out on an angle. Use a 1 × 2 plate between the bottom of the mouth and the head.

2x
4539097

1x
6122504

1x
6001609

2x
6072998

1x
74335

4x
4539082

1x
6028736

1x
4213568

2x
302321

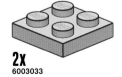
1x
4585751

2x
6003033

1x
6073040

2x
6127601

4x
4619815

2x
4541498

2x
4282860

1x
6097402

SPRITE

1 2x 1x

2 1x 1x

3 2x 2x

4 1x 1x

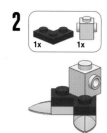

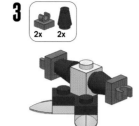

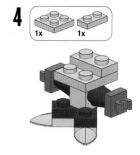

5 1x 2x

6 2x 2x

7 2x 2x

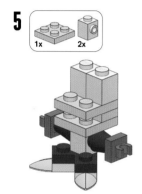

8 2x 1x

9 2x 1x

10 1x 1x

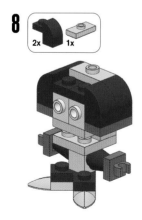

BattleR

BattleR was made for the battlefield—its guns are hoisted and ready to fire. Its red eyes are also weapons—they can shoot laser beams out of them! This robot has a thick-plated armor that makes it hard for enemy fire to penetrate. When building your brick version of this machine, attach each gun to the body using a 2 × 2 round tile with an open stud. Use click hinges to join the legs and give the robot more support.

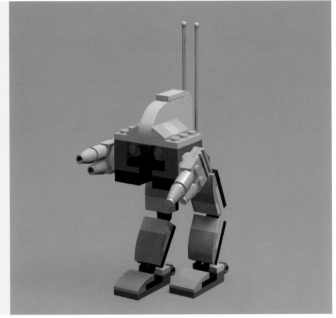

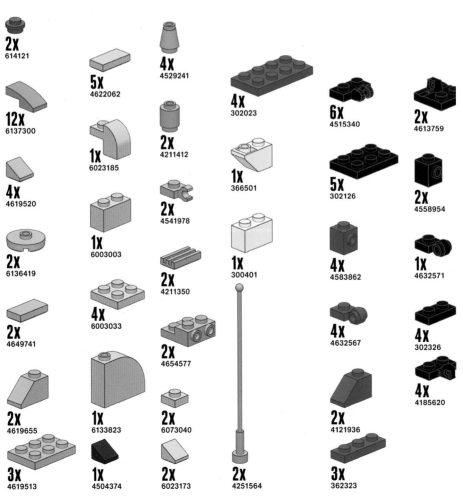

2x 614121

12x 6137300

4x 4619520

2x 6136419

2x 4649741

2x 4619655

3x 4619513

5x 4622062

1x 6023185

1x 6003003

4x 6003033

1x 6133823

4x 4529241

2x 4211412

2x 4541978

2x 4211350

2x 4654577

1x 4504374

4x 302023

1x 366501

1x 300401

1x 6073040

2x 6023173

6x 4515340

5x 302126

4x 4583862

4x 4632567

1x 4251564

2x 4613759

2x 4558954

1x 4632571

4x 302326

4x 4185620

2x 4121936

3x 362323

2x 6073040

2x 4251564

BATTLER

1
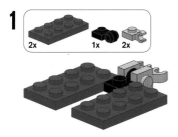

2
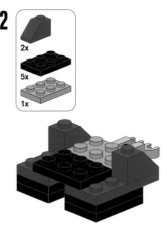

3

4
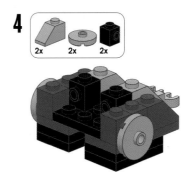

5
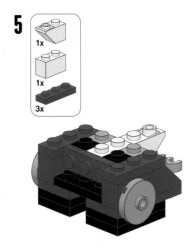

6
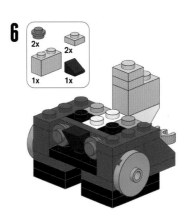

7

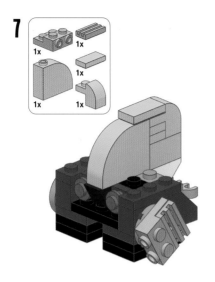

8

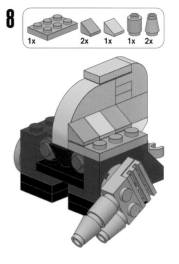

9

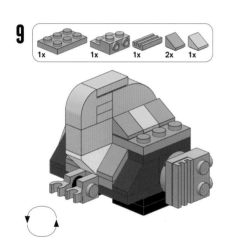

10

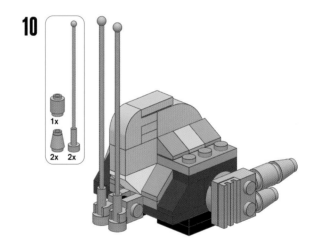

11

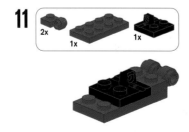

12

BATTLER

13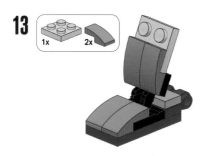

14

15

16

MAKE 2

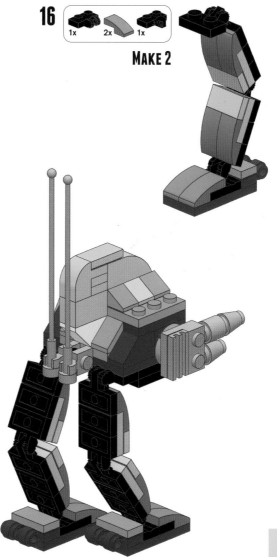

17

Lo-Tech

"It wasn't me!" exclaims Lo-Tech. Large, wide eyes and a gaping mouth create the shocked expression of this clumsy creature. It's a real klutz! It means well and tries to be helpful, but it is always bumping into things and knocking them over. It's just as well there are on and off buttons on its front. Build your version using 2 × 2 round tiles with a hole so a 1 × 1 round plate can be placed inside—this creates those large eyes. Use 1 × 1 round bricks for its skinny arms and legs.

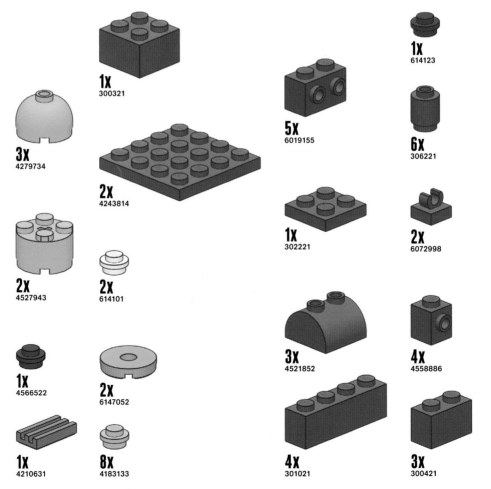

1X
614123

1X
300321

3X
4279734

5X
6019155

6X
306221

2X
4243814

2X
4527943

2X
614101

1X
302221

2X
6072998

1X
4566522

2X
6147052

3X
4521852

4X
4558886

1X
4210631

8X
4183133

4X
301021

3X
300421

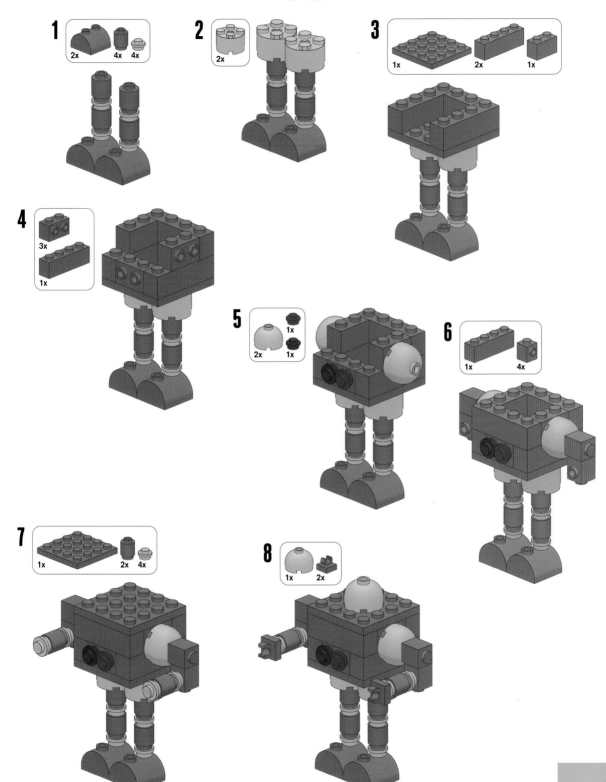

9

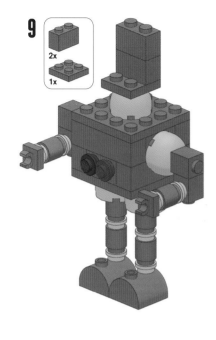

10

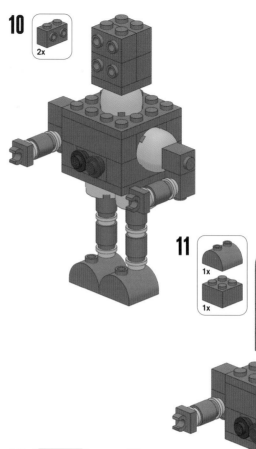

11

12

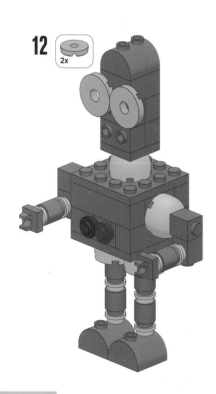

13

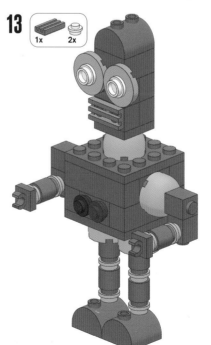

Budd EE

Budd EE is the best robot friend you could have. It is a gentle giant with big eyes—and a very big smile. Just like a pet dog, Budd EE is always overjoyed to see you. But beware—it has a very healthy appetite, as you can tell by its very large tummy. Build this spherical robot body using 4 x 4 round corner bricks, also known as macaroni bricks. Use a red plate and red tile for its big red lips, and 1 x 2 curved slopes for its claws.

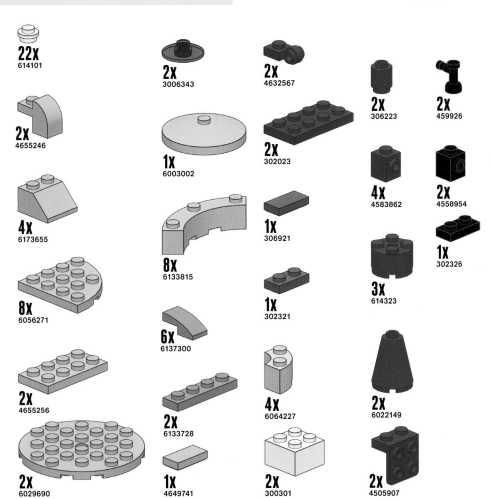

22x
614101

2x
3006343

2x
4632567

2x
306223

2x
459926

2x
4655246

1x
6003002

2x
302023

4x
4583862

2x
4558954

4x
6173655

8x
6133815

1x
306921

1x
302326

8x
6056271

1x
302321

3x
614323

6x
6137300

2x
4655256

2x
6133728

4x
6064227

2x
6022149

2x
6029690

1x
4649741

2x
300301

2x
4505907

55

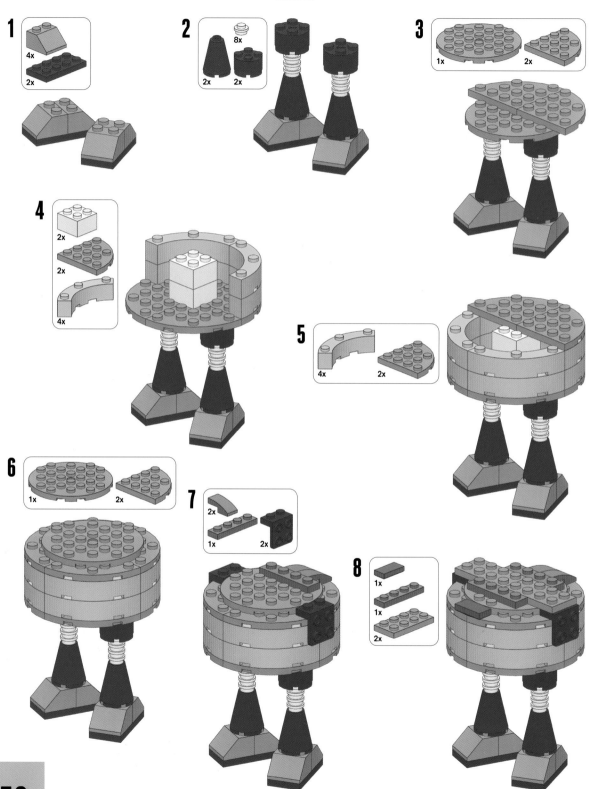

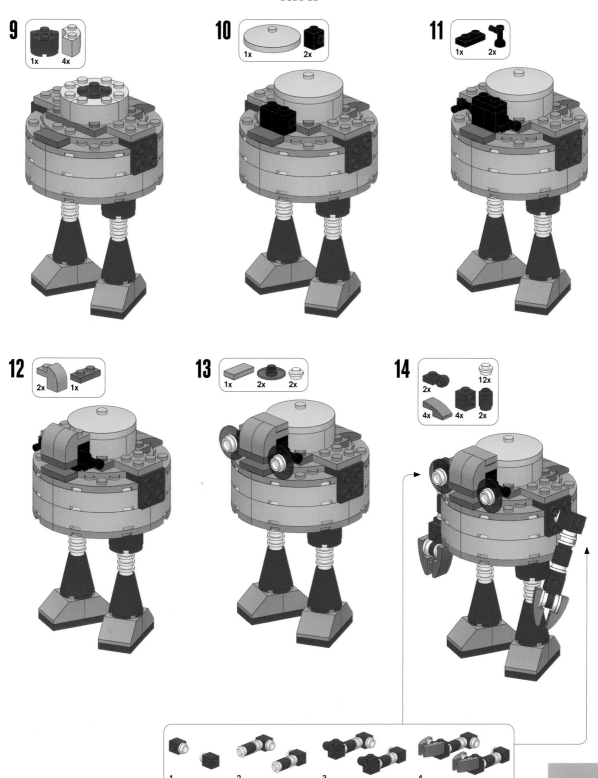

Dis K

Don't mess with this little ninja! Dis K means business—and is very good at its job as a spy. It moves around on four wheels so quietly, you won't hear it sneaking about. It will then stop suddenly and hide behind its shields to avoid being seen. Create your brick Dis K using 4 x 4 radar dishes on each side and on top for the shields. For the two side dishes, use plates with clips and handles to allow each arm to extend out and close in.

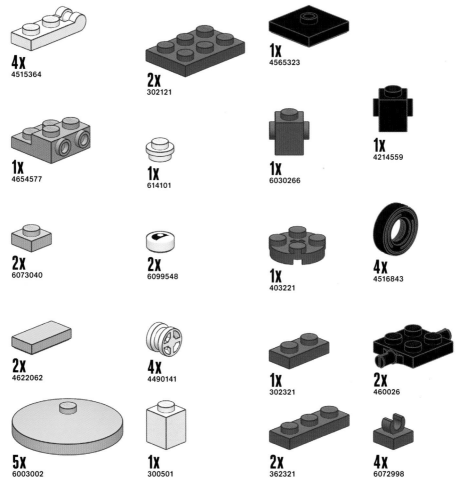

4x
4515364

2x
302121

1x
4565323

1x
4654577

1x
614101

1x
6030266

1x
4214559

2x
6073040

2x
6099548

1x
403221

4x
4516843

2x
4622062

4x
4490141

1x
302321

2x
460026

5x
6003002

1x
300501

2x
362321

4x
6072998

DIS K

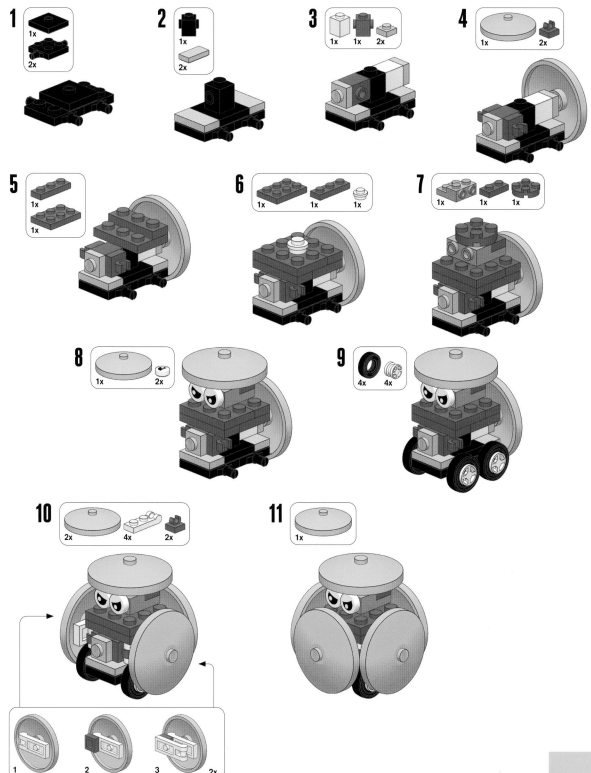

Bolt

The spiderlike Bolt is a scary creepy-crawly. It moves at lightning speed as it tiptoes up behind you and taps you on the shoulder—and boy will that give you a fright! Build this red robot using a 1 × 2 plate with clips for its insectoid mouth, and two dome lever bases to make the eyes look like they are squinting. Use plates with clips and handles for its bendy legs, and attach cones to their ends for its pointed feet.

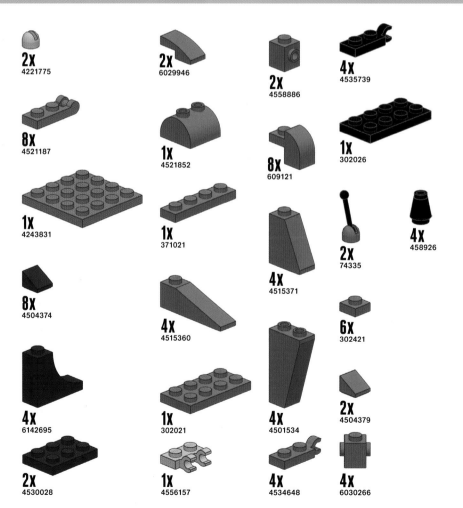

2x 4221775

2x 6029946

2x 4558886

4x 4535739

8x 4521187

1x 4521852

8x 609121

1x 302026

1x 4243831

1x 371021

4x 4515371

2x 74335

4x 458926

8x 4504374

4x 4515360

6x 302421

4x 6142695

1x 302021

4x 4501534

2x 4504379

2x 4530028

1x 4556157

4x 4534648

4x 6030266

BOLT

1
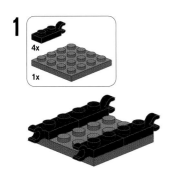

2
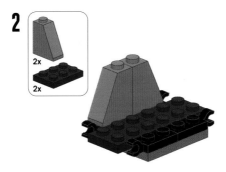

3
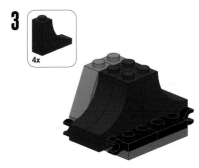

4
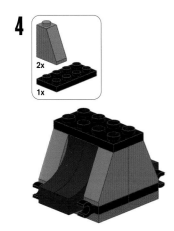

5
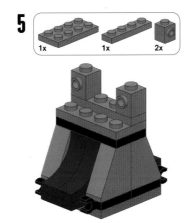

6

7

8
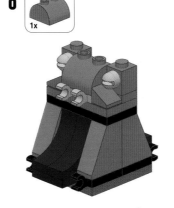

9
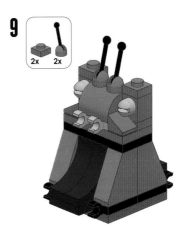

10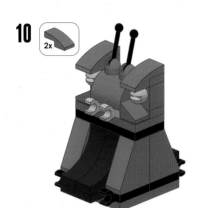

11

12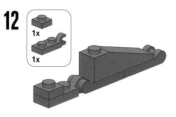

13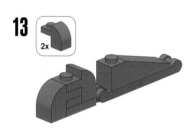

14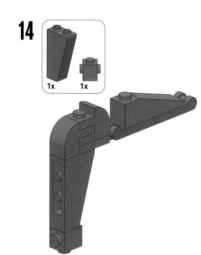

15 MAKE 4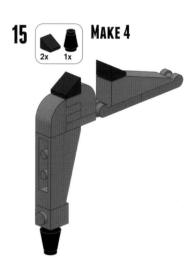

16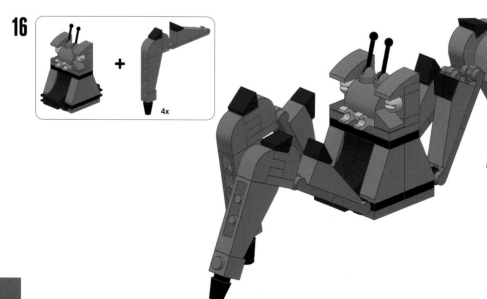

Gizmo

Gizmo is very gentle and kind, and is always happy to make friends. It is a very useful friend to have, too, as there is no tech problem it can't solve! Build this LEGO® robot using bricks with studs on the side for the head so the large eyes can be attached—as can the orange curved slopes on the side, which form the pigtails in its hair.

1x
6030266

2x
6172869

1x
6061692

2x
6020106

1x
6115115

1x
6029690

2x
4515364

4x
4504371

1x
6092599

2x
6112356

1x
6115115

2x
4251969

2x
6003007

1x
487121

1x
6103415

2x
4540040

2x
614101

2x
6060734

1x
394201

3x
6072998

2x
4558886

1x
302321

1x
6019155

1x
302221

1x
371021

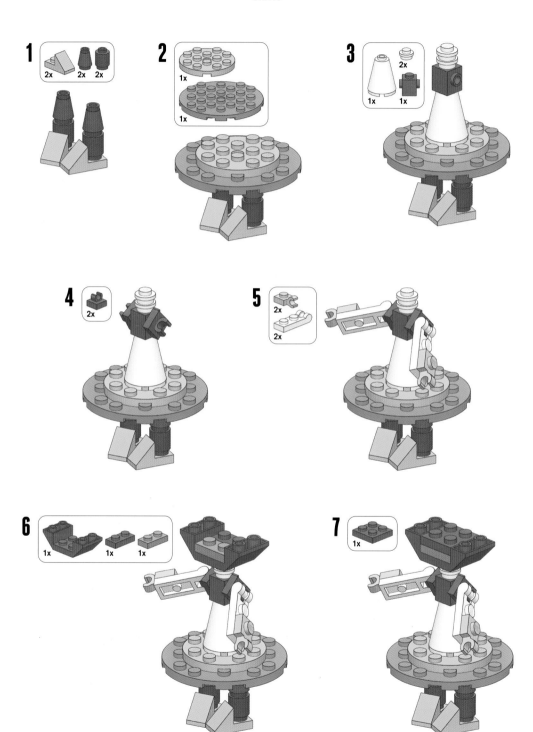

GIZMO

8
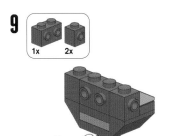
1x 2x

9
1x 2x

10
2x 2x

11
1x 2x

12
1x
2x
1x

Signal

Signal is an evolved version of a transistor radio. It still looks a little old-fashioned, but it can walk around and tune in to any station you ask it to. The satellite dish on its head can pick up signals from many miles away. Build your own version of Signal using log bricks to give the main part of its body a unique look. Use 1 x 2 curved bricks on top to give it a rounded-off finish. Attach one leg farther forward to create the illusion that it is walking.

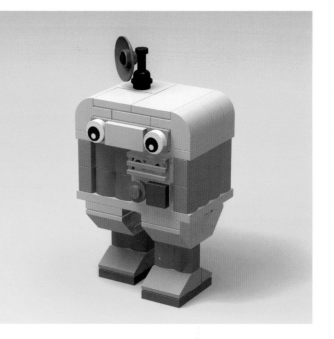

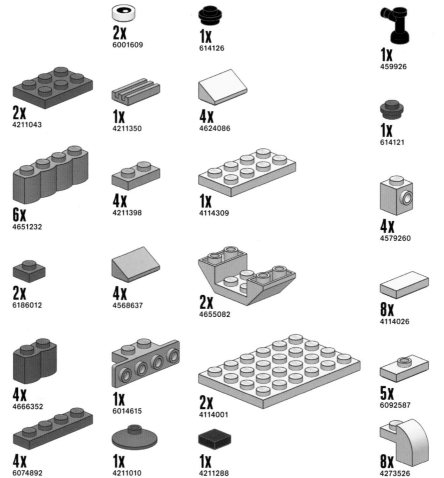

2x 6001609

1x 614126

1x 459926

2x 4211043

1x 4211350

4x 4624086

1x 614121

6x 4651232

4x 4211398

1x 4114309

4x 4579260

2x 6186012

4x 4568637

2x 4655082

8x 4114026

4x 4666352

1x 6014615

2x 4114001

5x 6092587

4x 6074892

1x 4211010

1x 4211288

8x 4273526

SIGNAL

1
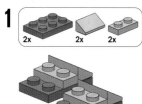
2x 2x 2x

2

2x
2x 2x

3
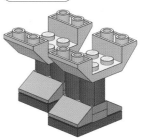
2x

4
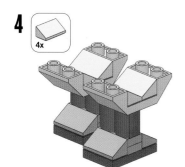
4x

5
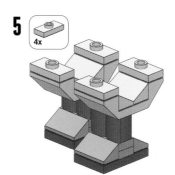
4x

6
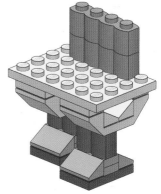
1x 2x

7
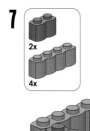
2x
4x

8
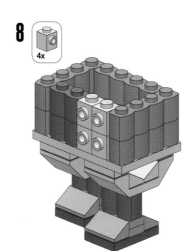
4x

9
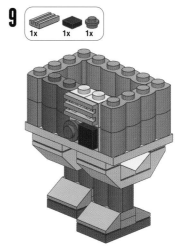
1x 1x 1x

10
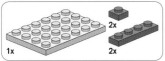

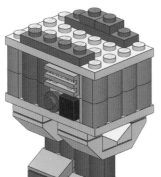

11

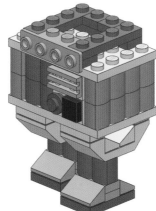

12

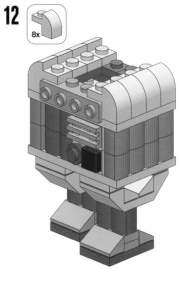

13
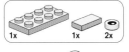

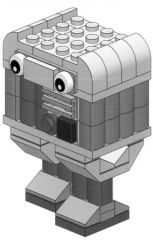

14

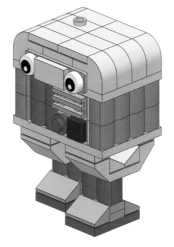

15

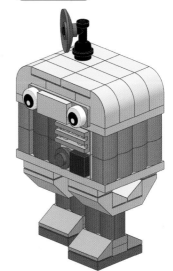

Tin Byte

Tin Byte is reaching for the stars! Its entire body is made like a rocket that is ready to blast into outer space. It has a pointed head, wide triangular feet from which blasters will launch it sky-high, and wings on its back so it can fly around. Create Tin Byte's wings by attaching the orange wedge plates to the blue plate using only one stud—this allows them to rotate up and out. Use different-sized cones to give the robot's head a sleek aerodynamic look.

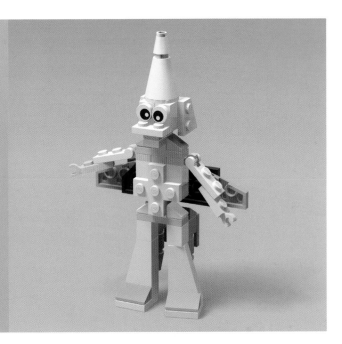

2x
4521921

1x
4180540

1x
302301

1x
302401

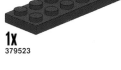
1x
241923

2x
4213567

1x
4180512

2x
4515364

2x
4504369

1x
379523

2x
4211350

1x
4118782

2x
302201

10x
4558952

2x
4540040

2x
6073040

1x
4580007

1x
6099412

1x
394201

2x
4535740

2x
6023173

2x
4529241

1x
302101

1x
4518400

1x
6132203

4x
6073042

2x
4211412

3x
6068996

2x
446001

2x
6001609

1x
6132204

TIN BYTE

1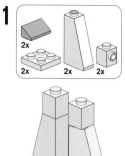

2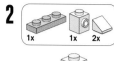

3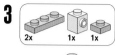

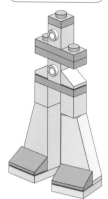

4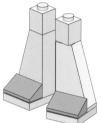

5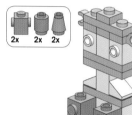

6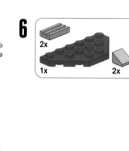

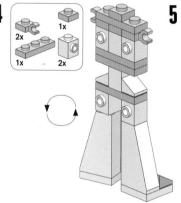

7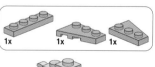

8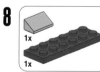

9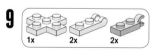

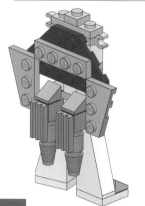

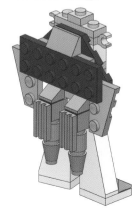

10 2x

11 1x 1x 1x

12 1x 2x

13 2x 1x 1x

14 1x 1x 2x

15

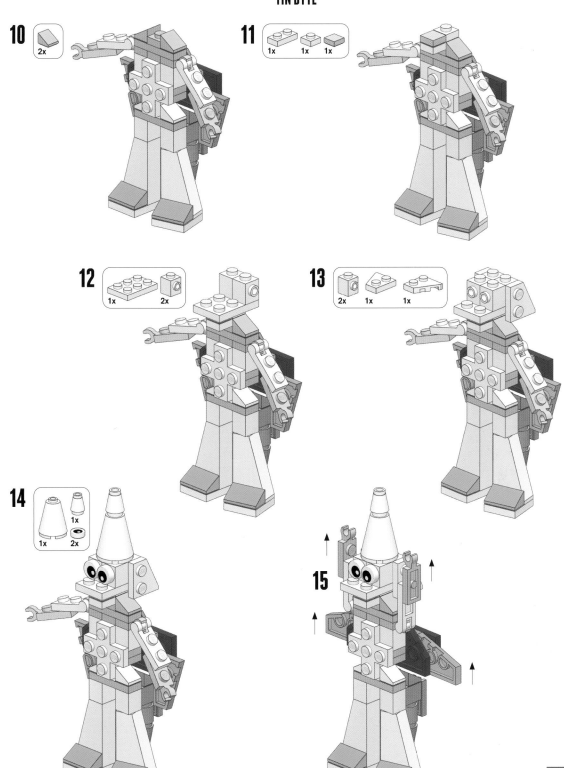

Wheels

Decked out in army combat colors, Wheels is ready for battle. This brick soldier robot is built in the shape of a tank on wheels, with its head peeking out of the top. Build several of these characters to form your own army battalion. Use two shades of green and tan for the various bricks and slopes to create the great camouflage pattern. Slide an antenna into the round bricks to strengthen the barrel of the gun.

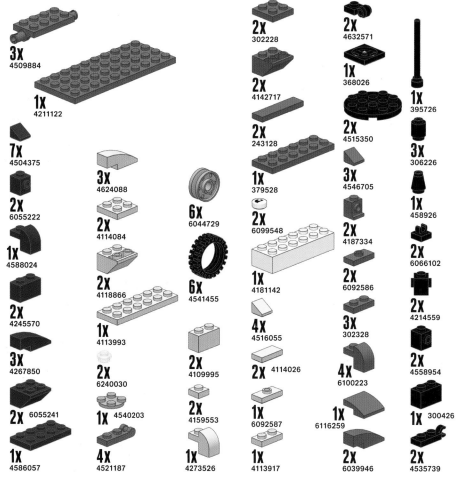

3x 4509884

1x 4211122

7x 4504375

2x 6055222

1x 4588024

2x 4245570

3x 4267850

2x 6055241

1x 4586057

3x 4624088

2x 4114084

2x 4118866

1x 4113993

2x 6240030

1x 4540203

4x 4521187

6x 6044729

6x 4541455

2x 4109995

2x 4159553

1x 4273526

2x 302228

2x 4142717

2x 243128

1x 379528

2x 6099548

1x 4181142

4x 4516055

2x 4114026

1x 6092587

1x 4113917

2x 4632571

1x 368026

2x 4515350

3x 4546705

2x 4187334

2x 6092586

3x 302328

4x 6100223

1x 6116259

2x 6039946

1x 395726

3x 306226

1x 458926

2x 6066102

2x 4214559

2x 4558954

1x 300426

2x 4535739

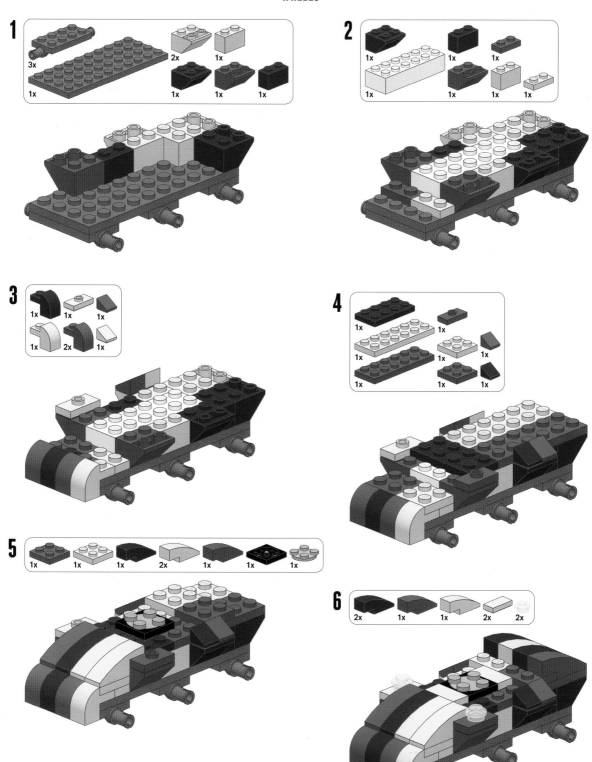

7

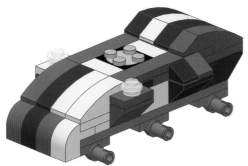

8

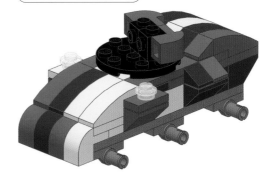

9

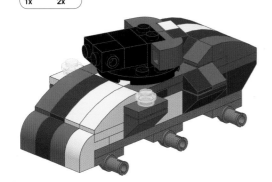

10

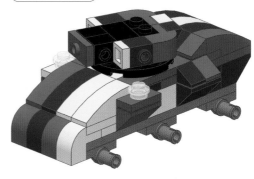

11

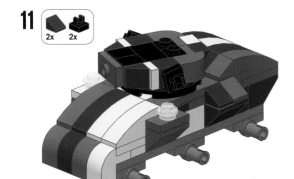

12

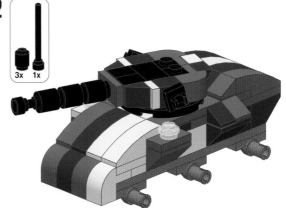

13

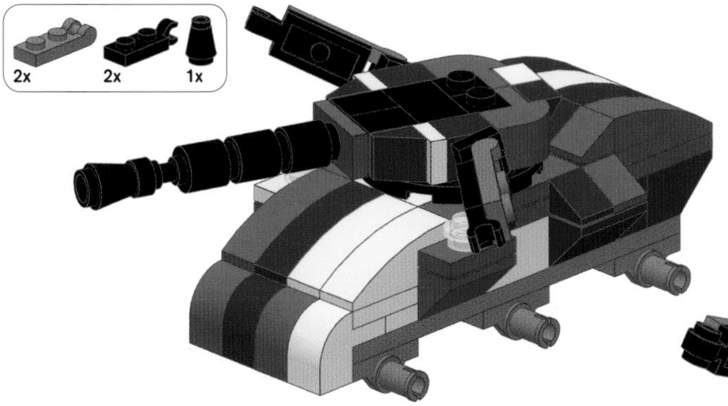

2x 2x 1x

14

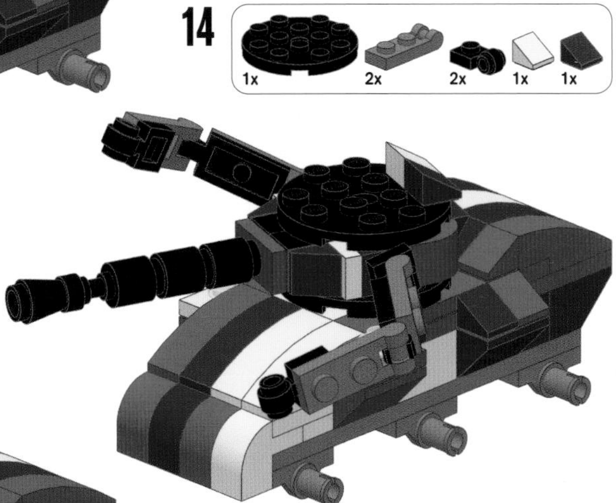

1x 2x 2x 1x 1x

15

2x 2x

16

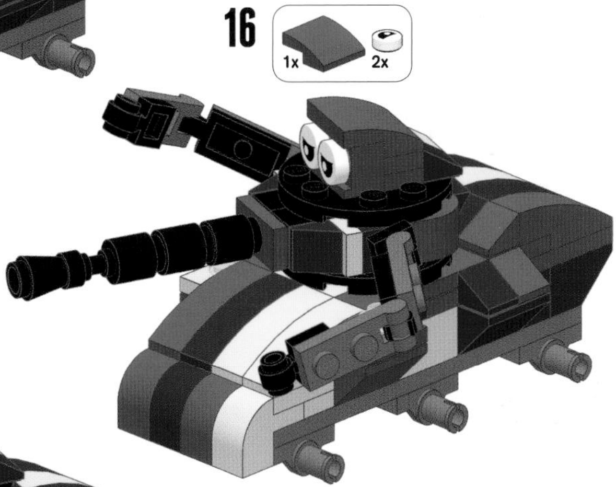

1x 2x

17

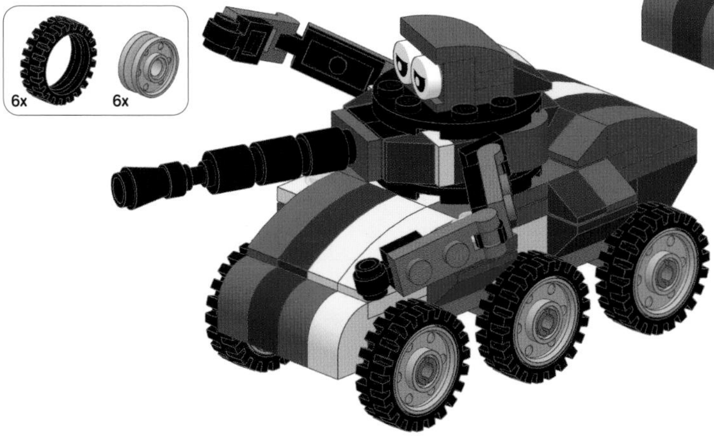

6x 6x

Jump

Is it a bus? Is it a mailbox? No, it's Jump! This is no ordinary robot—it is a superhero, with superhuman strength; just look at those biceps! Jump uses its round, flat feet to spring high into the air, and covers large distances to catch the bad guys. Build these feet by connecting 3 × 3 radar dishes to the legs using a bar with mechanical claw. Attach the legs to Technic bricks in the body, which allows them to pivot back and forth.

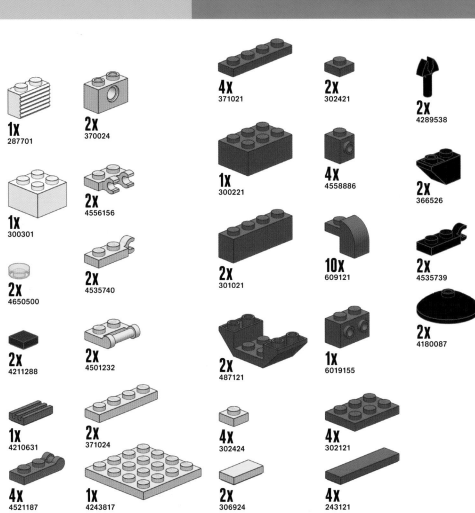

1x 287701

2x 370024

1x 300301

2x 4556156

2x 4650500

2x 4535740

2x 4211288

2x 4501232

1x 4210631

2x 371024

4x 4521187

1x 4243817

4x 371021

1x 300221

2x 301021

2x 487121

4x 302424

2x 306924

2x 302421

4x 4558886

10x 609121

1x 6019155

4x 302121

4x 243121

2x 4289538

2x 366526

2x 4535739

2x 4180087

JUMP

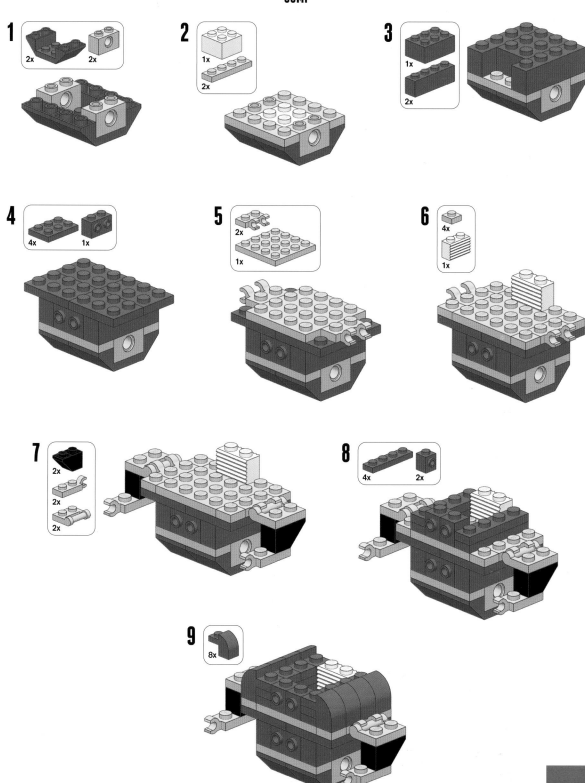

10 4x

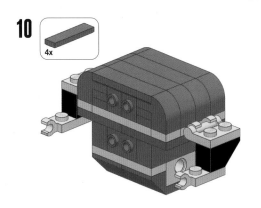

11 1x 2x

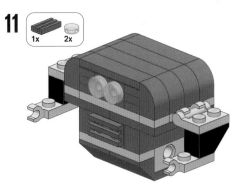

12 2x 2x 2x

13 2x 2x 2x

14 2x 2x

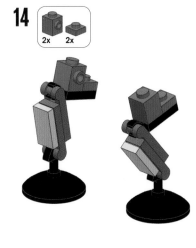

15 2x 2x

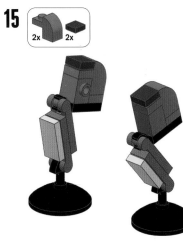

16

+

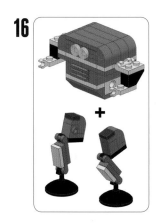

Moto 2

This clever innovator has made itself a propeller contraption so it can fly around the world. It is permanently on vacation and loves nothing more than discovering new and exciting places. Build your Moto 2 robot using a 1 × 6 × 2 curved top arch brick for the legs—this will keep it stable when it lands. Connect the rotor section to the hands using a bar to keep it in place. Position a 1 × 2 jumper plate under the head to give the robot a chin.

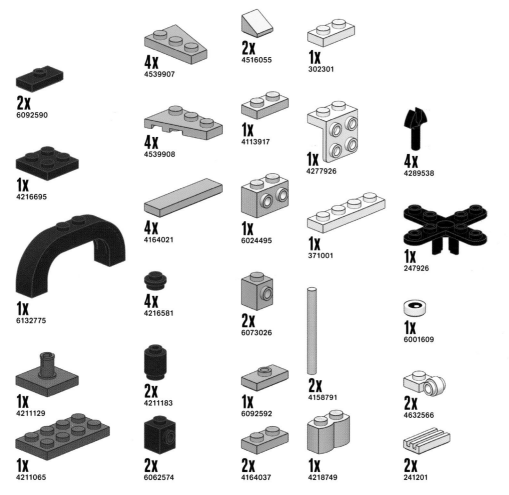

2x 6092590

1x 4216695

1x 6132775

4x 4539907

4x 4539908

4x 4164021

4x 4216581

2x 4516055

1x 4113917

1x 6024495

2x 6073026

1x 302301

1x 4277926

1x 371001

1x 6001609

4x 4289538

1x 247926

1x 4211129

2x 4211183

1x 6092592

2x 4158791

2x 4632566

1x 4211065

2x 6062574

2x 4164037

1x 4218749

2x 241201

79

MOTO 2

1

2

3

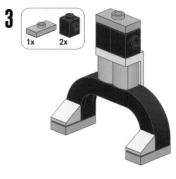

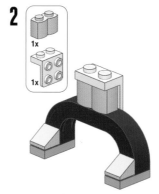

4

5

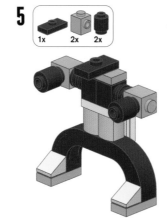

6

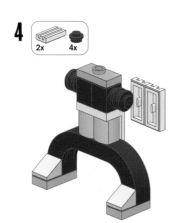

7

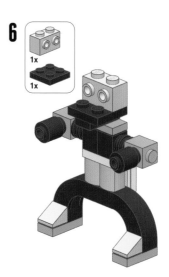

8

9

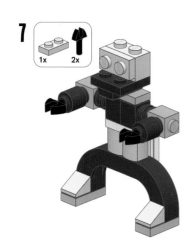

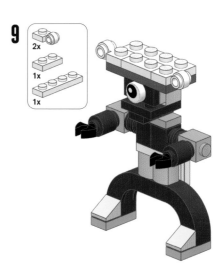

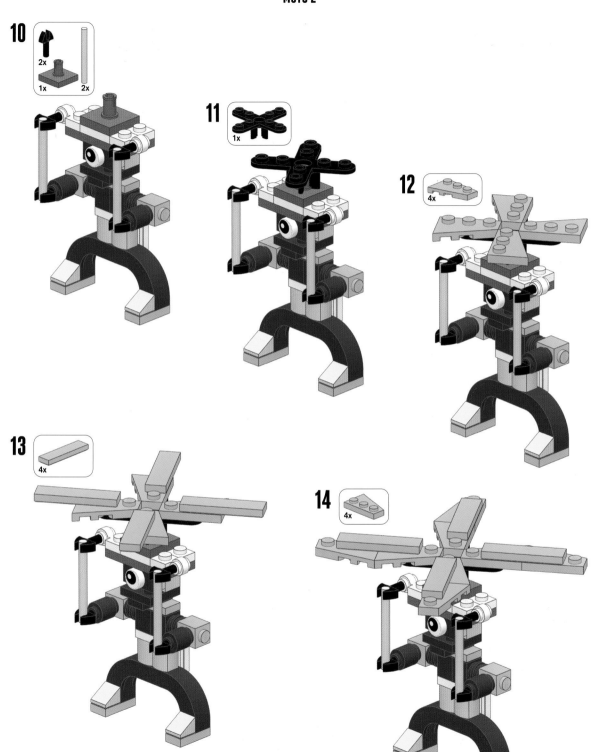

BracKIT

BracKIT is a droid mechanic that has the tools for every task. This rotund robot keeps these gadgets safely tucked away inside its body, but you can see some of them sticking out from its sides. Build your BracKIT using the SNOT (Studs Not On Top) technique—this creates a ball shape for the body. Attach 1 x 1 bricks with studs on all sides to each side of the body and the top of the ball. Use 1 x 2 jumper plates to connect the different tools to the sides.

3x
6122504

1x
368021

1x
4289538

1x
6003033

2x
6001609

2x
302421

1x
459926

2x
6115115

1x
4221775

5x
306921

1x
459926

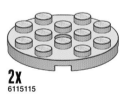

4x
4539082

1x
4540203

2x
6019155

8x
473326

20x
4585751

5x
4622062

7x
4243814

1x
74335

82

BRACKIT

1
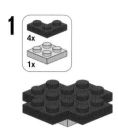

4x
1x

2
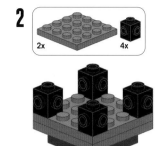

2x
4x

3
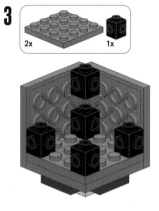

2x
1x

4
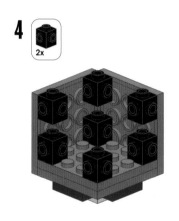

2x

5
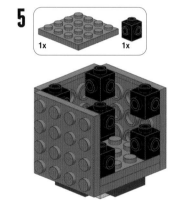

1x
1x

6
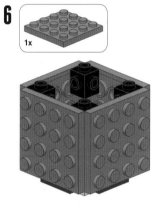

1x

7
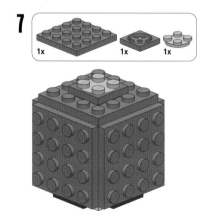

1x
1x
1x

8
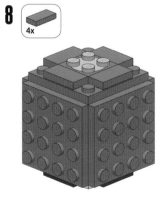

4x

9
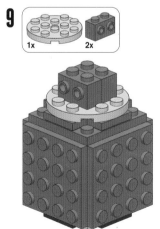

1x
2x

10

2x 1x 2x

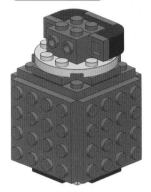

11

2x 2x

12
1x 1x

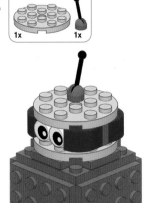

13
8x

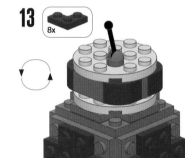

14
3x
1x 1x

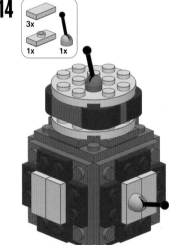

15
8x

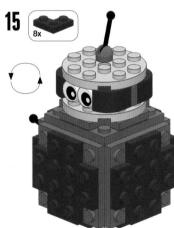

16
2x
2x 1x 1x

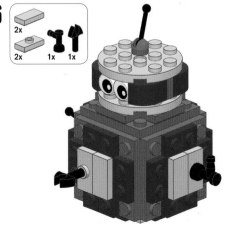

Feeder

Feeder is your convenient snack vending machine robot. Shaped a little bit like a gingerbread man, Feeder will boil, bake, roast, grill, or fry whatever food you're craving and dispense it from the middle of its tummy. Build this brick robot using windows to see the item inside the body. Create the head using 1 × 2 curved bricks, with the bottom section upside down and attached using bricks with studs on the side. Use 1 × 1 plates with lamp holders for the forearms.

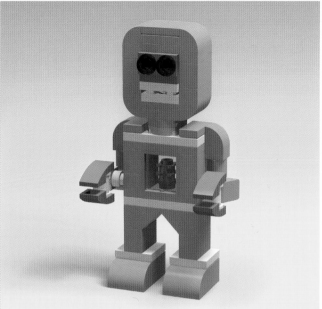

2x
6149782

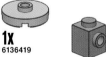
2x
4619520

1x
4216581

1x
302201

2x
4619599

2x
6019155

2x
4625032

1x
6136419

2x
6004938

4x
614101

2x
6240214

2x
6070756

4x
4649741

1x
4653988

1x
371001

1x
302001

2x
302401

4x
4632566

2x
6146866

10x
4655246

4x
6137300

1x
6147052

4x
379401

2x
4655256

8x
6092674

2x
4620909

2x
4537946

2x
302301

FEEDER

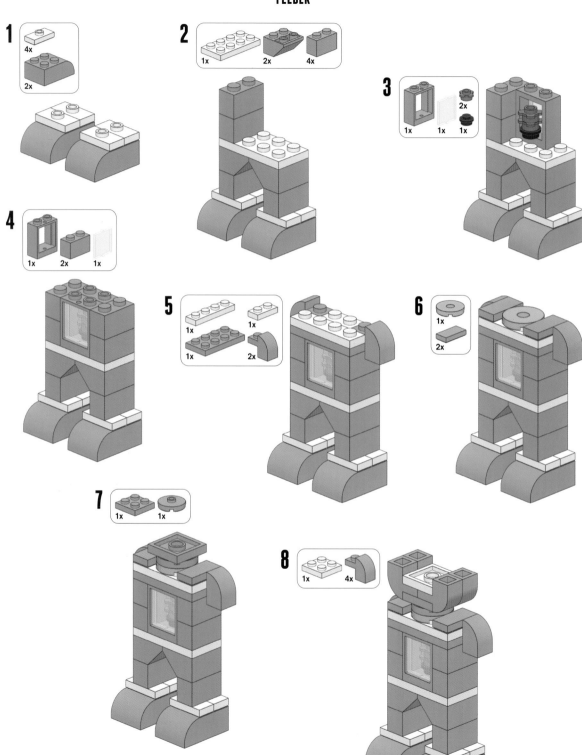

FEEDER

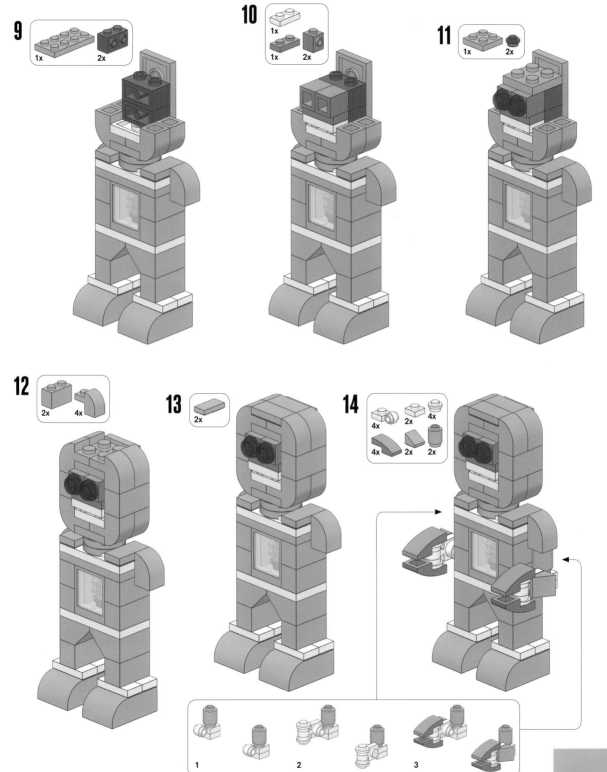

Flyte

The birdlike Flyte robot wants to be the fastest-flying robot in the world! It will practice for hours on end, flying around and around. Its beak points the way and its arms are raised in flight. Create this little creature using a 2 × 2 octagonal plate with bar frame for the main body. Then attach the wings, tail, and head to it so that they can all move up and down. Use a triple slope attached to a bracket to give the impression of a beak.

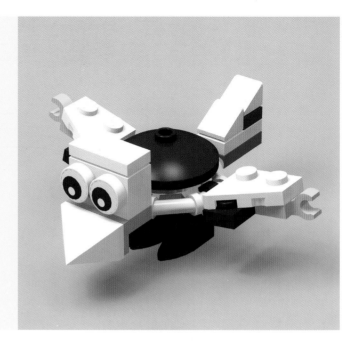

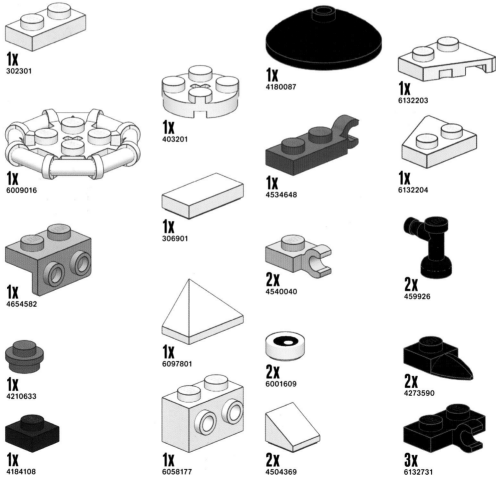

1X 302301

1X 403201

1X 4180087

1X 6132203

1X 6009016

1X 306901

1X 4534648

1X 6132204

1X 4654582

2X 4540040

2X 459926

1X 4210633

1X 6097801

2X 6001609

2X 4273590

1X 4184108

1X 6058177

2X 4504369

3X 6132731

FLYTE

1

2x 2x

2
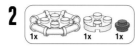
1x 1x 1x

3

3x

1x

4
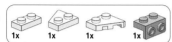
1x 1x 1x 1x

5

2x 1x 1x

6

1x 1x

7

1x

1x

8

1x 2x

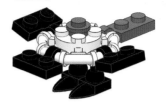

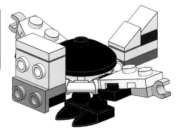
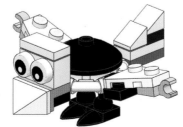

Romudroid

Romudroid is the ultimate robotic gladiator from mythological times— it even has wings on its helmet. This character is tough and was built to compete. Build your version using bricks and plates in steps from bottom to top to create the cylindrical body. Use Technic bricks to connect the arms to the body, and connect the 2 × 2 round bricks for the legs using 1 × 1 round plates placed between the studs.

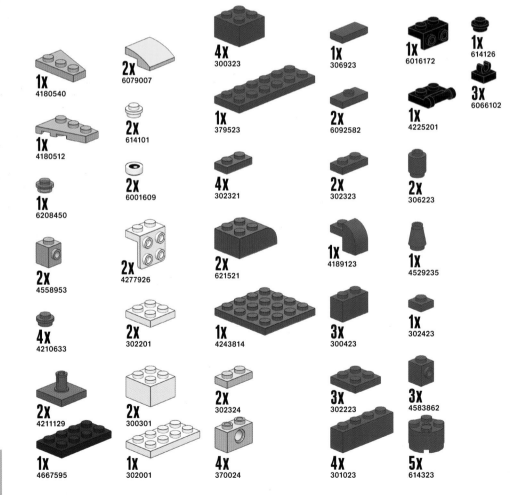

1x 4180540

2x 6079007

4x 300323

1x 306923

1x 6016172

1x 614126

1x 4180512

2x 614101

1x 379523

2x 6092582

1x 4225201

3x 6066102

1x 6208450

2x 6001609

4x 302321

2x 302323

2x 306223

2x 4558953

2x 4277926

2x 621521

1x 4189123

1x 4529235

4x 4210633

2x 302201

1x 4243814

3x 300423

1x 302423

2x 4211129

2x 300301

2x 302324

3x 302223

3x 4583862

1x 4667595

1x 302001

4x 370024

4x 301023

5x 614323

ROMUDROID

1
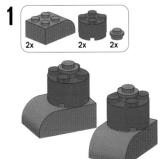
2x 2x 2x

2
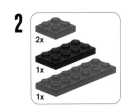
2x
1x
1x

3
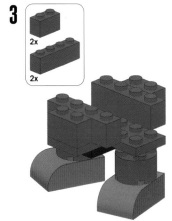
2x
2x

4
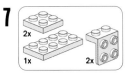
1x 2x 2x

5
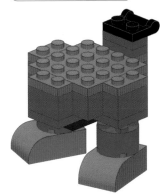
1x
1x
2x
2x

6
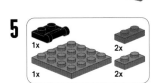
1x 2x
2x 1x 1x

7

2x
1x 2x

8
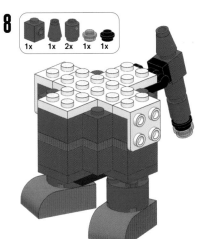
1x 1x 2x 1x 1x

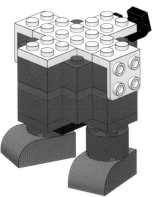

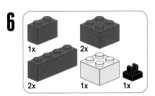

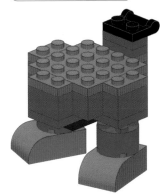

91

ROMUDROID

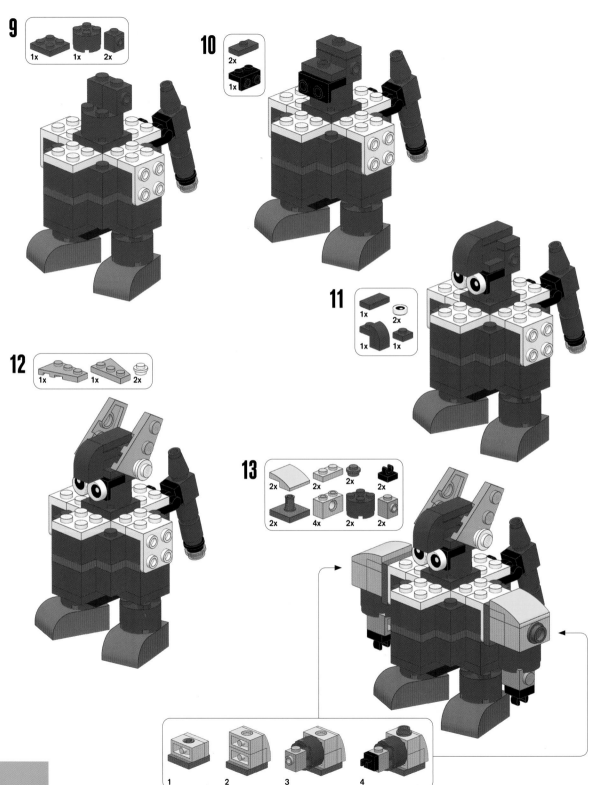

Amah

If you're looking for a robot nanny, you have found it in Amah. This gentle robot is shaped a bit like a sofa so that baby robots can sit on its knee while it hums lullabies. It's also pretty good at knitting. Create your brick Amah robot's arms using bar holders with handles attached to bars with mechanical claws—this allows them to be moved and positioned. Use two levers for the knitting needles.

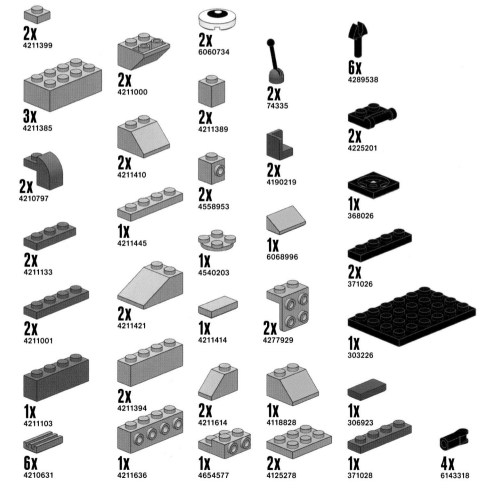

2x 4211399

3x 4211385

2x 4210797

2x 4211133

2x 4211001

1x 4211103

6x 4210631

2x 4211000

2x 4211410

1x 4211445

2x 4211421

2x 4211394

1x 4211636

2x 6060734

2x 4211389

2x 4558953

1x 4540203

1x 4211414

2x 4211614

1x 4654577

2x 74335

2x 4190219

1x 6068996

2x 4277929

1x 4118828

2x 4125278

6x 4289538

2x 4225201

1x 368026

2x 371026

1x 303226

1x 306923

1x 371028

4x 6143318

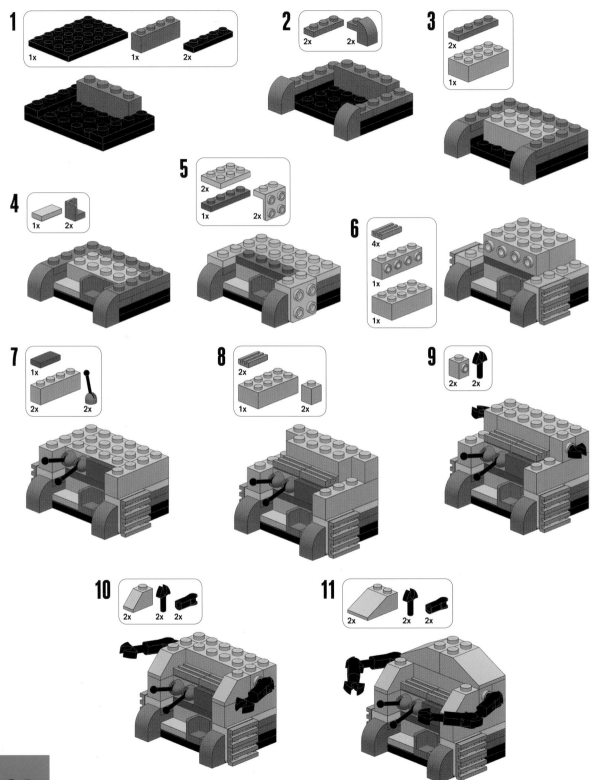

12

1x
1x
2x

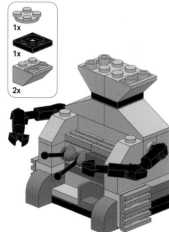

13

2x
1x

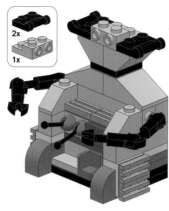

14

2x
1x

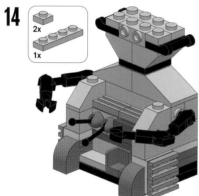

15

2x

16

2x
1x
1x

Glossary

Here are some of the more unusual LEGO® pieces that you'll find in this book:

Arch brick

Click hinge

Clip

Corner brick

Corner plate

Curved brick

Curved slope

Inverted slope

Jumper plate

Lamp holder

Lever

Plate with a handle
on the end

Plate with a handle
on the side

Radar dish

Round dome brick

Skateboard wheel

Tooth plate/brick

Triple slope

Wedge

Wedge plate